Activities Manual
to accompany

Looking Out / Looking In
SEVENTH EDITION

Ronald Adler
Neil Towne

Prepared by
Mary O. Wiemann
Santa Barbara City College

Harcourt Brace Jovanovich College Publishers

Fort Worth   Philadelphia   San Diego   New York   Orlando   Austin   San Antonio
Toronto   Montreal   London   Sydney   Tokyo

ISBN: 0-03-094055-9

Address Editorial Correspondence To: Harcourt Brace Jovanovich, Inc.
301 Commerce Street, Suite 3700
Fort Worth, Texas 76102

Address Orders To: Harcourt Brace Jovanovich, Inc.
6277 Sea Harbor Drive
Orlando, Florida 32887
1-800-782-4479 or 1-800-433-0001 (in Florida)

Printed in the United States of America

2 3 4 5 6 7 8 9 0 1   0 1 8   9 8 7 6 5 4 3 2 1

CONTENTS

CHAPTER 7   LISTENING: MORE THAN MEETS THE EAR

Outline   173

Vocabulary Terms   175

CHAPTER 8   INTIMACY AND DISTANCE IN RELATIONSHIPS

Outline   202

Vocabulary Terms   203

CHAPTER 9   IMPROVING COMMUNICATION CLIMATES

Outline   229

Vocabulary Terms   230

CHAPTER 10   MANAGING INTERPERSONAL CONFLICTS

PREFACE

This Activities Manual contains over one hundred class-tested exercises designed to build understanding of principles and proficiency in skills introduced in *Looking Out/Looking In*, Sixth Edition.

Extended outlines and vocabulary terms for each chapter precede the exercises; they help students study for exams and focus on important concepts and terms.

The activities are arranged to parallel the chapters in the text and are printed on perforated pages to allow easy duplication for student use.

Students who complete the exercises in this manual will develop understanding and skill in each area through a sequence of activities, including:

Class/Group activities—designed primarily to help students identify the target behavior in a number of common interpersonal communication situations. They also provide group activities to reinforce learning in the classroom.

Assignment activities—designed to give students opportunities to develop proficiency in a newly learned skill. They are designed to be done out of class and are usually written.

Journal activities—designed to help students discover how newly learned principles can be applied in their everyday lives. They can be grouped together to form a "Communication Journal" for the entire course.

Oral Skill activities—designed to allow students to actually exhibit communication behaviors they have studied. They are designed for individual, dyadic, or small group use in a classroom or lab setting.

Practice test activities—designed to help students identify major concepts or skills contained in the chapter. They are designed to be done individually, in groups, or with the entire class, and they have answer keys to them found in the back of the manual.

Many of the activities can be used in a variety of ways. Instructors can adapt them, use some or all, grade them or leave them ungraded, assign them all as out-of-class exercises, or use them all as class enrichment. Student observations in many exercises will lead to class discussions on how to apply the newly learned principles in the "real world" of one's interpersonal relationships.

While they almost always stimulate class discussion, the activities in this manual are designed to do more than keep a class busy or interested. If they are used regularly, they will help students to move beyond simply understanding the principles of interpersonal communication and actually to perform more effectively in a variety of communication situations.

M.O.W.

CHAPTER ONE

▲ A First Look ▲

▲ I. **INTRODUCTION TO THE STUDY OF INTERPERSONAL COMMUNICATION**
   A. **Communication Is Important**
   B. **We Communicate to Satisfy Needs**
      1. Physical needs
      2. Identity needs
      3. Social needs (Rubin)
         a. Pleasure
         b. Affection
         c. Inclusion
         d. Escape
         e. Relaxation
         f. Control
      4. Practical needs (Maslow's categories)
         a. Physical
         b. Safety
         c. Social
         d. Self-esteem
         e. Self-actualization

II. **THE PROCESS OF COMMUNICATION**
   A. **A Linear View**
      1. Sender
      2. Encoding
      3. Message
      4. Channel
      5. Decoding
      6. Receiver
      7. Noise
         a. External
         b. Physiological
         c. Psychological

B. **An Interactive View**
   a. Feedback
   b. Environments
   c. Discrete "acts"

C. **A Transactional View**
   a. Send/receive messages simultaneously
   b. Non-isolated "acts"

III. **COMMUNICATION PRINCIPLES AND MISCONCEPTIONS**
   A. **Communication Principles**
      1. Communication can be intentional or unintentional
      2. It's impossible not to communicate
      3. Communication is irreversible
      4. Communication is unrepeatable

   B. **Avoiding Communication Misconceptions**
      1. Meanings are not in words
      2. More communication is not always better
      3. Communication will not solve all problems
      4. Communication is not a natural ability

IV. **INTERPERSONAL AND IMPERSONAL COMMUNICATION**
   A. **Distinguished by the Quality of Interaction**
      1. Interpersonal treats people as unique
      2. Impersonal treats people more like objects

   B. **Distinguished by Characteristics**
      1. Uniqueness
      2. Irreplaceability
      3. Interdependence
      4. Disclosure
      5. Intrinsic rewards
      6. Scarcity

   C. **Balancing Interpersonal and Impersonal Communication**

V. **COMMUNICATING ABOUT RELATIONSHIPS**
   A. **Content and Relational Messages**

   B. **Metacommunication**

   C. **Types of Relational Messages**
      1. Affinity
      2. Respect
      3. Control
         a. Types
            (1) Decision
            (2) Conversational

b. Distribution
(1) Complementary
(2) Symmetrical
(3) Parallel

VI. **COMMUNICATION COMPETENCE: WHAT MAKES AN EFFECTIVE COMMUNICATOR?**
A. **Communication Competence Defined**
1. No "ideal" way to communicate
2. Competence is situational
3. Competence has a relational dimension
B. **Characteristics of Competent Communication**
1. A wide range of behaviors
2. The ability to choose the most appropriate behavior
a. Context
b. Your goal
c. The other person
3. Skill at performing behaviors
a. Beginning awareness
b. Awkwardness
c. Skillfulness
d. Integration
e. Empathy/perspective-taking
f. Cognitive complexity
g. Self-monitoring
4. Commitment to the relationship
a. Commitment to the other person
b. Commitment to the message
c. A desire for mutual benefit
d. A desire to interact and to continue the relationship

▲ KEY TERMS

affection
affinity
awareness
awkwardness
channel
commitment
communication
communication competence
communication misconceptions
communication model
communication principles
competitive symmetry
complementary relationship
content message

context
control
conversational control
decision control
decoding
dyad
dyadic communication
encoding
environment
escape
feedback
impersonal communication
inclusion
influence

integration
interactive communication model
interpersonal communication
interpersonal relationship
intimacy
linear communication model
message
metacommunication
needs (physical, identity, social, practical)
neutralized symmetry
noise (external, physiological, psychological)

parallel relationship
pleasure
receiver
relational message
relaxation
self-actualization
self-monitoring
sender
skillfulness
symmetrical relationship
transactional communication model

▲ 1.1 COMMUNICATION SKILLS INVENTORY

PURPOSES

1. To help you discover how satisfied you are with the way you communicate in various situations.
2. To preview some topics that will be covered in *Looking Out/Looking In.*

INSTRUCTIONS

1. Below you will find several communication-related situations. As you read each item, imagine yourself in that situation.
2. For each instance, answer the following question: *How satisfied am I with the way I would behave in this situation and ones like it?* You can express your answers by placing one of the following numbers in the space by each item:

   5 = Completely satisfied with my probable action
   4 = Generally, though not totally, satisfied with my probable action
   3 = About equally satisfied and dissatisfied with my probable action
   2 = Generally, though not totally, dissatisfied with my probable action
   1 = Totally dissatisfied with my probable action

_____ 1. A new acquaintance has just shared some personal experiences with you that make you think you'd like to develop a closer relationship. You have experienced the same things and are now deciding whether to reveal these personal experiences. (8)

_____ 2. You've become involved in a political discussion with someone whose views are the complete opposite of yours. The other person asks, "Can't you at least understand why I feel as I do?" (3, 7)

_____ 3. You are considered a responsible adult by virtually everyone except one relative who still wants to help you make all your decisions. You value your relationship with this person, but you need to be seen as more independent. You know you should do something about this situation. (9, 10)

_____ 4. In a mood of self-improvement a friend asks you to describe the one or two ways by which you think he or she could behave better. You're willing to do so, but need to express yourself in a clear and helpful way. (3, 5, 10)

_____ 5. A close companion says that you've been behaving "differently" lately and asks if you know what he or she means. (5, 6, 7)

_____ 6. You've grown to appreciate a new friend a great deal lately, and you realize that you ought to share your feelings. (4)

_____ 7. An amateur writer you know has just shown you his or her latest batch of poems and asked your opinion of them. You don't think they are very good. It's time for your reply. (5, 9, 10)

_____ 8. You've found certain behaviors of an important person in your life have become more and more bothersome to you. It's getting harder to keep your feelings to yourself. (4, 10)

_____ 9. You're invited to a party or other event at which everyone except the host will be a stranger to you. Upon hearing about this, a friend says, "Gee, if I were going I'd feel like an outsider. They probably won't have much to do with you." How do you feel? (2)

_____ 10. A friend comes to you feeling very upset about a recent incident and asks for advice. You suspect that there is more to the problem than just this one incident. You really want to help the friend. (7)

_____ 11. You find yourself defending the behavior of a friend against the criticisms of a third person. The critic accuses you of seeing only what you want to see and ignoring the rest. (2, 4, 5, 9, 10)

_____ 12. A boss or instructor asks you to explain a recent assignment to a companion who has been absent. You are cautioned to explain the work clearly so there will be no misunderstandings. (5)

_____ 13. You ask an acquaintance for help with a problem. She says yes, but the way the message is expressed leaves you thinking she'd rather not. You do need the help, but only if it's sincerely offered. (6, 10)

_____ 14. A roommate always seems to be too busy to do the dishes when it's his or her turn, and you've would up doing them most of the time. You resent the unequal sharing of responsibility and want to do something about it. (10)

_____ 15. A new acquaintance has become quite interested in getting to know you better, but you feel no interest yourself. You've heard that this person is extremely sensitive and insecure. (1, 2)

You can use the results of this survey in two ways. By looking at each question you can see how satisfied you are with your behavior in that specific type of situation. A response of 1 or 2 on any single question is an obvious signal that you can profit from working on that situation. Parenthetical numbers following each item indicate the chapters of _Looking Out/Looking In_ which focus on that subject.

By totaling your score for all of the items you can get an idea of how satisfied you are with your overall ability to communicate in interpersonal situations. A score of 68–75 suggests high satisfaction, 58–67 indicates moderate satisfaction, while 45–57 shows that you feel dissatisfied with your communication behavior nearly half the time.

Another valuable way to use this activity is to make a second inventory at the end of the course. Have you improved? Are there still areas you will need to work on?

▲ 1.2 EXPANDING YOUR COMMUNICATION EFFECTIVENESS

PURPOSES

1. To help you broaden your repertoire of effective communication behaviors and your skill at performing them.
2. To help you identify the most appropriate communication behaviors in important situations.

INSTRUCTIONS

1. Use the space below to identify two areas in which you would like to communicate more effectively.
2. For each area, identify a person you have observed who communicates in a way that you think would improve your effectiveness. Describe this person's communication behavior.
3. Describe how you could adapt these behaviors to your own life.

EXAMPLE

a. Area in which you would like to communicate more effectively
   Making conversation with people I've just met.
b. Model who communicates effectively in this area *My friend Rich*
c. Model's behavior *He asks sincere questions of people he's just met, compliments them enthusiastically, and smiles a lot.*
d. How could you apply these behaviors? *I can spend more time thinking about people I've just met and less time thinking self-consciously about my own nervousness. Then I can focus on parts of these new people that interest me and let the other person know I'm interested. The key seems to be sincerity: I have to really mean what I say and not use questions and compliments as tricks.*

SITUATION 1

a. Area in which you would like to communicate more effectively

   _____

b. Model who communicates effectively in this area _____

c. Model's behavior _____

   _____

d. How could you apply these behaviors? _____

   _____

   _____

   _____

SITUATION 2

    a. Area in which you would like to communicate more effectively

    _____

    b. Model who communicates effectively in this area _____

    c. Model's behavior _____

    _____

    d. How could you apply these behaviors? _____

    _____

    _____

    _____

SITUATION 3

    a. Area in which you would like to communicate more effectively

    _____

    b. Model who communicates effectively in this area _____

    c. Model's behavior _____

    _____

    d. How could you apply these behaviors? _____

    _____

    _____

    _____

▲ 1.3 BARRIERS TO EFFECTIVE COMMUNICATION

PURPOSES

1. To help you understand barriers to effective communication in order to broaden your repertoire of effective communication behaviors and your skill at performing them.
2. To help you understand the elements of the transactional communication model introduced in Chapter 1 of *Looking Out/Looking In*.

INSTRUCTIONS

For each element of the communication model listed below, identify two personal experiences in which the element created a problem for one of your important relationships.

MESSAGE

EXAMPLE

Person(s) involved *My boss*
The problem *He calls me "honey" when he asks me to do something. I'm bothered by that word and his patronizing tone of voice.*

EXPERIENCE 1

Person(s) involved _____

The problem _____

EXPERIENCE 2

Person(s) involved _____

The problem _____

CHANNEL

EXAMPLE

Person(s) involved *My friend Carol*
The problem *She drops by to chat without phoning first to see if I'm busy. This forces me to be rude sometimes.*

EXPERIENCE 1

Person(s) involved _____

The problem _____

EXPERIENCE 2

Person(s) involved _____

The problem _____

NOISE (EXTERNAL, PHYSIOLOGICAL, OR PSYCHOLOGICAL)

EXAMPLE

Person(s) involved _My sister_
The problem _She often tries to talk to me while watching her favorite television shows, and she keeps sneaking glances at the screen._

EXPERIENCE 1

Person(s) involved _____

The problem _____

EXPERIENCE 2

Person(s) involved _____

The problem _____

DIFFERING ENVIRONMENTS

EXAMPLE

Person(s) involved _My parents_
The problem _Whenever we discuss raising a family, they keep focusing on their experiences, which are different from mine._

EXPERIENCE 1

Person(s) involved _____

The problem _____

EXPERIENCE 2

Person(s) involved _____

The problem _____

IRREVERSIBILITY OF COMMUNICATION

EXAMPLE

Person(s) involved _My friend Rebecca_
The problem _Once I jokingly kidded her about being fat, and she took it seriously. Now I can't convince her I think she looks just fine._

EXPERIENCE 1

Person(s) involved _____

The problem _____

EXPERIENCE 2

Person(s) involved _____

The problem _____

▲ 1.4 RECOGNIZING RELATIONAL MESSAGES

PURPOSES

1. To demonstrate that virtually every message has both a content and a relational dimension.
2. To give you practice recognizing the relational dimension of common messages.
3. To demonstrate that relational message are ambiguous and need to be verified by perception checking statements.

INSTRUCTIONS

Describe the relational issues that seem to be involved in each of the situations listed below.

Content Level	Relational Level (Inclusion, Control, Affection, Respect)
Example: *Students and instructor disagree about whether testing and grading system is fair.*	**Control:** *Students' right to help shape course.* **Respect:** *Whether instructor values opinions of students.*
1. A friend asks if you want to come over and share a bottle of wine.	
2. Wife complains that husband doesn't help out enough around the house.	
3. Boss asks your opinion about making changes in business.	
4. Couple argues about whose family to visit over holidays.	
5. Friend A teases friend B in good-natured way about B's bad memory.	
6. Employees object to management's requirement that all illnesses be verified by a doctor's note.	

Content Level	Relational Level (Inclusion, Control, Affection, Respect)
7. Several old acquaintances call to ask if you'll be attending a high school reunion.	
8. Roommate sighs, grimaces, and says "all right" when you ask for a ride.	
9. Parents remind teenager to drive carefully every time s/he goes out.	
10. Doctor's receptionist puts you on hold for five minutes when you call to make an appointment.	
11. Roommate nods, smiles and says, "Sure, that's a great idea."	
12. Student asks the professor, "Can you suggest any more books on that subject?"	
13. Parent says to college student, "You have to come home for the holidays! Everybody wants to see you!"	
14. "We really must get together sometime," a co-worker says with enthusiasm.	

▲ 1.5 EVALUATING YOUR COMMUNICATION COMPETENCE

PURPOSES

1. To clarify the situational, relational nature of communication competence.
2. To identify your communication competence in an important relationship.

INSTRUCTIONS

1. Identify one relationship that is important to you.
2. Evaluate your communication competence in this relationship according to the following directions.
3. Answer the questions at the end of the exercise.

SEE CHART ON PAGE 15

1. Name of other person _____

2. Relationship to you (friend, brother, etc.) _____

Situation	Range of Behaviors		Ability to Choose Most Appropriate Behavior		Skill at Performing Behavior	
	Yours	Other's	Yours	Other's	Yours	Other's
Example: My boyfriend Joe and I argue over whether we should move in together or not.	I really have one style of arguing—I get my feelings hurt and tend to pout.	Joe has a larger range of behaviors. He can be rational and logical but then gets very emotional at times.	I need to choose some other behaviors—pouting isn't getting us anywhere.	Joe probably chooses his behaviors more carefully. He can tell when his extremely logical reasoning really gets to me, so he will give me a hug or smile and make a joke of our predicament.	Neither Joe or I have much skill in problem-solving. Both of us keep doing the same things over and over again. We need to learn some new skills to handle our impasse.	
1.						
2.						
3.						

Ability to View Issue from a Variety of Perspectives		Ability to Monitor Your Behavior While Communicating	Commitment to the Relationship	
Yours	Other's		Yours	Other's
I can see Joe's perspective pretty clearly; he worries about what his family thinks and he's very influenced by his religion. Both of those make it hard to move in with me before we're married.	I think Joe has a harder time seeing my perspective. Because his parents have been together all these years, he doesn't understand my reluctance (based on a very nasty divorce) to marry before we've tried living together.	Because I get so emotional when we argue, I don't monitor my behavior very well. It is only afterwards that I say, "I wish I hadn't said that" or "If only I'd . . ."	I'm very committed to this relationship. I like Joe's stability and I admire his morals.	Joe says he's committed to this relationship, too, but I think he has a stronger commitment to his family than I do.

1. Based on your observations in this exercise, when do you communicate competently? Consider settings (e.g., at home, with friends); topics (e.g., money, romance); emotions (e.g., affection, conflict).
2. When do you not communicate competently?
3. What role does your partner's communication competence play in the success of your relationships?

▲ 1.6 IDENTIFYING YOUR RELATIONAL MESSAGES

PURPOSE

To identify the important relational dimensions in the messages you send.

INSTRUCTIONS

1. Identify an important person with whom you will communicate frequently in the next few days.
2. Record eight instances in which you communicate with this person. For each instance, record
   a. the content dimension of your verbal message
   b. the significant nonverbal dimensions of your message
   c. the relational dimensions of your verbal and nonverbal messages
3. Answer the questions at the end of this exercise.

Name of person _____

Verbal Content of Message	Nonverbal Aspects of Message	Relational Dimensions of Message
Example Reminded roommate to pick up clothes at dry cleaners	Used superior, "parental" tone of voice; put my hands on my hips; stared while talking.	High control, low respect (implied roommate would probably forget); affinity dimension unclear—roommate knows I care but my manner probably indicated only a medium amount of affinity.
1.		
2.		
3.		
4.		

Verbal Content of Message	Nonverbal Aspects of Message	Relational Dimensions of Message
5.		
6.		
7.		
8.		

CONCLUSIONS

What are the most frequent types of relational messages you send to the person you chose for this exercise (e.g., high affinity, low respect, medium control)?

_____

_____

_____

How do you send these messages (cite both verbal and nonverbal channels)?

_____

_____

_____

Explain your level of satisfaction with the relational messages you send. How can you communicate the relational level more clearly?

_____

_____

_____

▲ 1.7 INTERPERSONAL AND IMPERSONAL COMMUNICATION

PURPOSES

1. To recognize the differences between interpersonal and impersonal communication.
2. To help you identify the needs that are filled or not filled as you communicate with others.

INSTRUCTION

1. Identify two people with whom you communicate regularly.
2. Record two instances in which you have communicated with each of these people.
3. Identify whether the communication was impersonal or interpersonal, using the definitions in Chapter 1 of *Looking Out/Looking In*.
4. Identify which category of categories of needs you were trying to fill in each instance: physical, ego, social (pleasure, affection, inclusion, escape, relaxation, control) or practical. Were the needs met?
5. Speculate about which category or categories of needs were or were not met for the other person.
6. Summarize your findings by answering the questions at the end of the exercise.

Situation	Impersonal/Interpersonal	Your Needs Met/Unmet	Others' Needs Met/Unmet
Example **Person:** My roommate, Lou. As usual, Lou was talking about his weight training program. I changed the subject to the party we're planning for the weekend.	Impersonal	I satisfied my need to plan for the party (control). Lou seemed a bit irritated at me for not listening to him. (affection)	I think Lou's desire for my respect wasn't met.
Person: 1. 2.			
Person: 1. 2.			

CONCLUSIONS

How much of your communication time with each of the above people is truly interpersonal? Describe how the examples you gave are typical of your communication with each person or whether other types of communication usually go on.

_____

_____

_____

_____

Is the degree of interpersonal communication in each of these relationships enough to satisfy your needs? Explain why or why not.

_____

_____

_____

_____

Does your style of communication usually satisfy the needs of the other people in your life? Explain why or why not.

_____

_____

_____

_____

▲ 1.8 CHECKLIST FOR ORAL SKILL— IDENTIFYING PERSONAL COMMUNICATION NEEDS

PURPOSES

1. To describe the differences between interpersonal and impersonal communication.
2. To describe the needs that were/were not filled in interpersonal and impersonal communication situations.

INSTRUCTIONS

Using *1.7 Interpersonal and Impersonal Communication* as a guide, prepare to deliver orally two short descriptions of communication situations in which you were involved.

1. Identify each situation as impersonal or interpersonal giving justification for your classification.
2. Describe your needs (physical, identity, social—pleasure, affection, inclusion, escape, relaxation, control—or practical) that were met or unmet by the situation. Explain how your needs fit into each category.
3. Describe your needs to a partner and then evaluate whether this message would or would not be effective in your relationship.
4. Describe the needs of your partner that were met or unmet by the situation, explaining how each need meets the definition of physical, identity, social (pleasure, affection, inclusion, escape, relaxation, control) or practical needs.

CHECKLIST

5 = superior   4 = excellent   3 = good   2 = fair   1 = poor

Speaks clearly and loud enough to be heard   _____

Makes eye contact with class members   _____

Describes and distinguishes two impersonal or interpersonal situations   _____

Describes personal needs that were met or unmet   _____

Describes personal needs to a partner   _____

Evaluates effectiveness of describing needs to a partner   _____

Describes needs of the other that were met or unmet   _____

                                                                                    Total   _____

▲ 1.9 ORAL SKILL IDENTIFYING CONTENT AND RELATIONAL MESSAGES

PURPOSE

To illustrate the content and relational messages of conversation.

INSTRUCTIONS

1. Videotape a 2–3 minute segment of *interaction* from a television program/movie that illustrates both the content and relational aspects of messages. Demonstrate how another relational message might be sent without altering the content aspect of the message.
   OR
   Prepare to act out with a partner a 2–3 minute segment of *interaction* from your own life, illustrating content and relational messages. Deliver the "content" message two ways by changing the relational message.
2. Play the videotape for the class or act out your own segment.
3. Identify the content and relational aspects of the messages contained in the interaction.
4. For each relational aspect, comment on the relational level (inclusion, control, affection, respect) and describe how that relational message affects the overall relationship.
5. Describe how you (or the actor in your videotape) might express the relational message verbally to a partner.

▲ 1.10 CHECKLIST FOR ORAL SKILL— IDENTIFYING CONTENT AND RELATIONAL MESSAGES

PURPOSE

To illustrate the content and relational aspects of messages.

INSTRUCTIONS

1. Using the situations videotaped or created in *1.9 Oral Skill—Identifying Content and Relational Messages*, deliver one to the class in two different ways by expressing the same content but altering it by sending two different relational messages.
2. Identify the content and relational aspects of both messages.
3. Identify the relational levels contained.
4. Express the relational message explicitly to a partner.
5. Comment on the effect of the relational message on the relationship, explaining why you would/would not send the relational message verbally in real life.

CHECKLIST

5 = superior   4 = excellent   3 = good   2 = fair   1 = poor

Prepares an interaction segment involving content/relational aspects
of messages and delivers the "content" two ways   _____

Identifies the content aspects of the messages   _____

Identifies the relational levels of the messages   _____

Expresses a relational message verbally to a partner   _____

Ties the effect of the relational message to the overall relationship,
explaining its impact   _____

                                                        Total   _____

▲ 1.11 IDENTIFYING THE COMMUNICATION PROCESS

PURPOSE

To give you practice in identifying elements of the communication process.

INSTRUCTIONS

1. Match the letter of the communication process element with its description found below. Underlined words provide clues.
2. Check your answers in the back of this manual on p. 281.
   a. encode
   b. decode
   c. channel
   d. message/feedback
   e. noise (external, physiological or psychological)
   f. environment

_____ 1. The children make a <u>videotape</u> of themselves to send to their grandparents instead of writing a <u>letter</u>.

_____ 2. Marjorie tries to decide the best way to tell Martin that she can't go to Hawaii with him.

_____ 3. Martin decides Marjorie means she doesn't love him when she says she can't go to Hawaii.

_____ 4. It's so hot in the room that Brad has a hard time concentrating on what his partner is telling him.

_____ 5. Linda <u>smiles</u> while Larry is talking to her.

_____ 6. Brooke is daydreaming about her date while Allison is talking to her.

_____ 7. Since Jacob has never been married, it's difficult for him to understand why his married friend Brent wants to spend less time with him.

_____ 8. Whitney says, "<u>I'm positive about my vote.</u>"

_____ 9. Richard <u>thinks</u> Jon wants to leave when he waves to him.

_____ 10. Laura <u>winks</u> when she <u>says</u> she's serious and <u>gestures</u> with her arms.

_____ 11. Erin is from a wealthy family and Kate from a poor one. They have a serious conflict about how to budget their money.

_____ 12. Jack has been feeling a cold coming on all day while he has sat through the meeting.

_____ 13. Levi constructs the best arguments to convince his parents to buy him a new car.

_____ 14. Jessica decides to lie to her group members about the reason she missed the meeting last night.

_____ 15. "I refuse to go," said Jeremy.

CHAPTER TWO

▲ Communication and the Self ▲

▲ **I. THE SELF-CONCEPT**

   A. Definition: The Set of Perceptions You Hold of Yourself

   B. How the Self-Concept Develops
1. Reflected appraisal (through significant others)
2. Social comparison (through reference groups)

   C. Characteristics of the Self-Concept
1. The self-concept is subjective
   a. Obsolete information
   b. Distorted feedback
   c. Emphasis on perfection
   d. Social expectations
2. High and low self-esteem affects relationships
3. The self-concept resists change
   a. Change-not-acknowledged problem
   b. Self-delusion/lack of growth problem

II. CULTURE AND THE SELF-CONCEPT

   A. Language

   B. Individualistic vs. Collective Identities

III. THE SELF-FULFILLING PROPHECY AND COMMUNICATION

   A. Definition: Expectations Held That Make an Outcome More Likely

   B. Types
1. Self-imposed
2. Imposed by others

   C. Influence
1. Improve relationships
2. Damage relationships

IV. CHANGING YOUR SELF-CONCEPT

    A. Have Realistic Expectations

    B. Have Realistic Perceptions

    C. Have the Will to Change

    D. Have the Skill to Change

V. PRESENTING THE SELF: COMMUNICATION AS IMPRESSION MANAGEMENT

    A. **Public and Private Selves**
       1. Perceived self
       2. Presenting self—facework

    B. **Roles—Strategies for Multiple Fronts**

    C. **Why Manage Impressions?**
       1. Social rules
       2. Personal goals
       3. Relational goals

    D. **How Do We Manage Impressions?**
       1. Manner
          a. Words
          b. Nonverbal behavior
       2. Appearance
       3. Setting

    E. **Honesty —The Ethics of Impression Management**

▲ KEY TERMS

appearance	obsolete information
back	perceived self
"can'ts"	presenting self
cognitive conservatism	reference groups
distorted feedback	reflected appraisal
ego booster	self-concept
ego buster	self-fulfilling prophecy
facework	self-monitor
front	setting
ideal self	significant other
impression management	social comparison
manner	social expectations
myth of perfection	"won'ts"

▲ 2.3 SELF-CONCEPT INVENTORY

PURPOSE

1. To give you a clearer picture of how you see yourself (your perceived self).
2. To illustrate how others perceive you (presenting selves).

INSTRUCTIONS

1. Transfer the list of self-concept descriptors found below to index cards (or strips of paper, or carefully cut the ones on this page). Feel free to line out some descriptors or add those of your own.
2. Arrange your cards in a stack, with the one that *best* describes you at the top and the one that *least* describes you at the bottom.
3. Using the Perceived Self column (Table 1), record the order in which you arranged the cards (1 is the most like you). You will leave out some cards or add on to your list on the opposite page.
4. Cover your Perceived Self column, and ask two other people (a friend, coworker, roommate, family member, classmate) to arrange the descriptors in an order in which they see you. Record these perceptions in Tables 2 and 3, being sure to cover your own Table 1 and the Table 2 or 3 that the other person has worked on (so no one sees what the other has written). Record the name/relationship of your evaluator at the top of the appropriate column.
5. Compare the three Tables, circling any descriptors that differ from column to column.
6. Answer the questions at the end of this exercise.

Intelligent	Constructive in personal relationships	Reliable
Shy	Satisfied with myself	Care about others
Express my feeling and ideas clearly	Comfortable in social situations	Tolerant
Give in easily	Confused	Honest with myself
Similar to other people	Friendly	Honest with others
Insecure	Emotionally mature	Make lots of excuses
Talk too much	Growing wiser over time	Avoid facing things
Helpful to others	Attractive	Good student and/or worker
Tense	Selfish	Athletic
Likeable	Conscientious	Organized
Open-minded	Willing to stand up for beliefs	Neat

Table 1 Perceived Self	Table 2 Presenting Self to	Table 3 Presenting Self to
	_____ (relationship to you)	_____ (relationship to you)
1. _____	1. _____	1. _____
2. _____	2. _____	2. _____
3. _____	3. _____	3. _____
4. _____	4. _____	4. _____
5. _____	5. _____	5. _____
6. _____	6. _____	6. _____
7. _____	7. _____	7. _____
8. _____	8. _____	8. _____
9. _____	9. _____	9. _____
10. _____	10. _____	10. _____
11. _____	11. _____	11. _____
12. _____	12. _____	12. _____
13. _____	13. _____	13. _____
14. _____	14. _____	14. _____
15. _____	15. _____	15. _____
16. _____	16. _____	16. _____
17. _____	17. _____	17. _____
18. _____	18. _____	18. _____
19. _____	19. _____	19. _____
20. _____	20. _____	20. _____
21. _____	21. _____	21. _____
22. _____	22. _____	22. _____
23. _____	23. _____	23. _____
24. _____	24. _____	24. _____

Describe any factors that have contributed in a positive or negative way to the formation of your perceived self (obsolete information, social expectations, perfectionistic beliefs). Include any other factors involved in the formation of your perceived self (for example, certain significant others, any strong reference groups).

_____

_____

_____

_____

_____

Describe any differences between your perceived self and the ways your evaluators perceived you (your presenting selves). What factors contribute to the differences in perception? Whose view is the most accurate and why?

_____

_____

_____

_____

_____

Why might your partners in this exercise view you differently from the way you perceive yourself? Would other people in your life view you like either of the people in this exercise? Give some specific examples with reasons why they would or would not have similar perception.

_____

_____

_____

_____

_____

▲ 2.4 REEVALUATING YOUR "CAN'TS"

PURPOSE

To help you identify and eliminate any self-fulfilling prophecies which hamper effective communication.

INSTRUCTIONS

1. Complete the following lists by describing communication-related difficulties you have in the following areas.
2. After filling in each blank space, follow the starred instructions that follow the list (*).

DIFFICULTIES YOU HAVE COMMUNICATING WITH FAMILY MEMBERS

EXAMPLES

I can't *discuss politics with my dad without having an argument*
because *he's so set in his ways.*
I can't *tell my brother how much I love him*
because *I'll feel foolish.*

1. I can't _____

   because _____

2. I can't _____

   because _____

* Corrections (see instructions at end of exercise)

_____

_____

DIFFICULTIES YOU HAVE COMMUNICATING WITH PEOPLE AT SCHOOL OR AT WORK

EXAMPLES

I can't *say "no" when my boss asks me to work overtime*
because *he'll fire me.*
I can't *participate in class discussions even when I know the answers or have a question*
because *I just freeze up.*

1. I can't _____

   because _____

2. I can't _____

   because _____

* Corrections (see instructions at end of exercise)

_____

_____

DIFFICULTIES YOU HAVE COMMUNICATING WITH STRANGERS

EXAMPLES

I can't *start a conversation with someone I've never met before*
because *I'll look stupid.*
I can't *ask smokers to move or stop smoking*
because *they'll get mad.*

1. I can't _____

   because _____

2. I can't _____

   because _____

* Corrections (see instructions at end of exercise)

_____

_____

DIFFICULTIES YOU HAVE COMMUNICATING WITH FRIENDS

EXAMPLES

I can't *find the courage to ask my friend to repay the money he owes me*
because *I'm afraid he'll question our friendship.*
I can't *say no when friends ask me to do favors and I'm busy*
because *I'm afraid they'll think I'm not their friend.*

1. I can't _____

   because _____

2. I can't _____

   because _____

* Corrections (see instructions at end of exercise)

_____

_____

*After you have completed the list, continue as follows:

a.   Read the list you have made. Actually say each item to yourself and note your feelings.

b.   Now read the list again, but with a slight difference. For each "can't," substitute the word "won't." For instance, "I can't say no to friends' requests" becomes "I won't say no." Circle any statements which are actually "won'ts."

c.   Read the list for a third time. For this repetition substitute "I don't know how" for your original "can't." Instead of saying "I can't approach strangers," say "I don't know how to approach strangers." *Correct* your original list to show which statements are truly "don't know hows."

After completing this exercise, you should be more aware of the power which negative self-fulfilling prophecies have on your self-concept and thus on your communication behavior. Imagine how differently you would behave if you eliminated any incorrect uses of the word "can't" from your thinking.

▲ 2.5 YOUR SELF-FULFILLING PROPHECIES

PURPOSES

1. To help you identify the self-fulfilling prophecies you impose on yourself.
2. To help you identify the self-fulfilling prophecies others impose on you.

INSTRUCTIONS

1. Identify three communication-related, self-fulfilling prophecies you impose on yourself. For each, identify the item, describe the prediction you make, and show how this prediction influences either your behavior or that of others.
2. Next, identify three communication-related, self-fulfilling prophecies others have imposed on you. For each, show how the other person's prediction affected your behavior.

PROPHECIES YOU IMPOSE ON YOURSELF

EXAMPLE

Item *Inept in social situations*
Prediction *When I'm at a party or other social gathering, I think about how foolish I'll sound when I meet strangers.*
Outcome *I do sound foolish when I meet them. I stammer, avoid eye contact, and can't think of anything interesting to say.*
How your prediction influenced outcome *I think that expecting to fail causes me to sound foolish. If I didn't expect to sound so foolish, I'd probably behave with more confidence.*

1. Item _____

   Prediction _____

   _____

   _____

   Outcome _____

   _____

   _____

   How prediction affected outcome _____

   _____

   _____

2. Item _____

   Prediction _____

   _____

   _____

   Outcome _____

   _____

   _____

   How prediction affected outcome _____

   _____

   _____

3. Item _____

   Prediction _____

   _____

   _____

   Outcome _____

   _____

   _____

   How prediction affected outcome _____

   _____

   _____

PROPHECIES OTHERS IMPOSE ON YOU

EXAMPLE

Item *Good listener*
Prediction *My friends often share their problems with me and tell me that I'm a good listener.*
Outcome *I'm willing to listen in the future.*
How prediction affected outcome *Being told I'm a good listener makes me more willing to lend an ear.*
If they told me I was no help, I'd probably discourage them from bringing me their problems in the future.

1. Item _____

   Prediction _____

   _____

   _____

   Outcome _____

   _____

   _____

   How prediction affected outcome _____

   _____

   _____

2. Item _____

   Prediction _____

   _____

   _____

   Outcome _____

   _____

   _____

   How prediction affected outcome _____

   _____

   _____

NAME _____

▲ 2.6. MANAGING IMPRESSIONS

PURPOSES

1. To illustrate the variety of faces that you can reveal to others.
2. To improve your self-monitoring ability.
3. To evaluate the strategic communication designed to influence another's perception of self.
4. To record your evaluation of the ethics of your impression management.

INSTRUCTIONS

1. In the columns below, record the aspects of your self that you have presented or would present in each of the situations.
2. Detail your manner and appearance and any aspects of the setting.
3. Answer the questions on managing impressions and ethics that follow.

Situation	Manner— verbal and nonverbal	Appearance— personal items	Setting— physical items
Example: You go to talk to your professor about your grades.	I adopted a more serious manner. I spoke clearly and listened intently. I took notes on what she told me. I sat upright.	I made sure my clothing was neat and clean. I combed my hair back and removed my sunglasses before I went in.	I got my books, quizzes and notebook ready before I went in so I would appear organized. I sat in the chair next to her desk.
1. You go to the doctor's office for a check up.			
2. You visit a grandparent.			

Situation	Manner— verbal and nonverbal	Appearance— personal items	Setting— physical items
3. You apply for a job.			
4. You go to the bank to get a loan.			
5. You decide to ask someone out for a date for the first time.			
6. You are going out for the first time with someone.			
7. A friend comes to your house to visit.			

Situation	Manner— verbal and nonverbal	Appearance— personal items	Setting— physical items
8. You're going out on Friday night with friends.			
9. You're telling a parent about how you're doing in school.			
10. You know you are going to have to introduce yourself to the class during the first week of class.			

Based on your ease or difficulty of completing this exercise, explain whether you are a high, medium or low self-monitor. Give other examples that illustrate your level of self-monitoring.

_____

_____

_____

_____

_____

_____

_____

How successful are you at creating desired impressions? Give examples not included above that illustrate your level of success in impression formation.

_____

_____

_____

_____

_____

_____

_____

How would you evaluate the honesty of your impression management techniques? Do you believe you are ethical in your approach? Give examples to support your evaluation.

_____

_____

_____

_____

_____

_____

_____

▲ 2.7 CHECKLIST FOR ORAL SKILL—MANAGING IMPRESSIONS

PURPOSE

To illustrate the ways you manage impressions with others.

INSTRUCTIONS

1. Using *2.6 Managing Impressions* as a starting point, consider the situations in which you present yourself in different ways. Choose two different ways you present yourself to others and explain how you present those aspects of yourself. Include aspects of your manner, appearance and setting. Explain your self-monitoring behaviors and evaluate the ethics of your impression management.
2. Use the checklist below to guide your evaluation of your impression management.

CHECKLIST

5 = superior   4 = excellent   3 = good   2 = fair   1 = poor

Makes eye contact with class   _____

Speaks in appropriate tone of voice   _____

Illustrates two examples of impression management   _____

Illustrates manner, appearance and setting   _____

Evaluates level of self-monitoring   _____

Evaluates ethics of impression management   _____

2.8 ORAL SKILL—REINFORCING POSITIVE SELF-CONCEPTS

PURPOSES

1. To practice acknowledging strengths.
2. To recognize and send upper messages.
3. To receive compliments.

INSTRUCTIONS

1. With a partner from class, tell one another the strengths you each have. You may acknowledge some weak aspects of your strengths, but you must focus on the strengths you perceive yourself to have and those you present in your presenting self.
2. Send positive messages to your partner, commenting on the strengths he/she presented to you or bringing up new strengths he/she may not have noticed that you have noticed about him/her.
3. Receive the compliments from your partner graciously, acknowledging the upper message sent ("thank you") or commenting on the validity of the upper message in a positive way ("Thank you, Jill, for saying you think I am probably honest; I am honest in my schoolwork and with my friends.")

▲ 2.9 CHECKLIST FOR ORAL SKILL—
REINFORCING POSITIVE SELF-CONCEPTS

PURPOSES

1. To acknowledge strengths.
2. To send positive messages.
3. To receive compliments.

INSTRUCTIONS

Using the situations developed in *2.8 Communicating Positive Self-Concepts*, converse about strengths, noting positive messages and receiving compliments. Do this for your instructor or videotape it.

CHECKLIST

5 = superior   4 = excellent   3 = good   2 = fair   1 = poor

Looks at partner appropriately   _____

Speaks in appropriate tone of voice   _____

Acknowledges personal strengths   _____

Delivers at least two positive messages to partner   _____

Accepts compliments graciously   _____

                                            Total   _____

▲ 2.10 IDENTIFYING ASPECTS OF THE SELF-CONCEPT

PURPOSE

To identify elements of the self-concept.

INSTRUCTIONS

1. Match the descriptions of the self with their labels below.
2. Check your answers in the back of this manual on page 281.

Identify which principle influences the self-concept in each example. Place the letter of the correct term on the line adjacent to each description.

    a. obsolete information
    b. distorted feedback
    c. emphasis on perfection
    d. social expectations

_____ 1. You always scored more points than anyone else on your team in high school. You still think you're the best even though your college teammates are scoring more than you.

_____ 2. You keep getting down on yourself because you can't cook as well as Megan, even though you are a great student and a fair athlete.

_____ 3. You tell everyone how you "blew" the chemistry test and got a "C–" but you don't ever acknowledge your "A's" in math.

_____ 4. Your parents tell you, their friends, and all your relatives about all your wonderful accomplishments, even though you have only average achievement.

_____ 5. Janee says that you are insensitive to her perspective despite your many attempts to honestly listen to her and empathize.

_____ 6. You pay a lot of attention to the magazines showing perfectly dressed and groomed individuals and keep wishing you could look as good as they do.

_____ 7. You think of yourself as the shy fifth grader despite being at the social hub of at least three clubs on campus.

_____ 8. You feel uncomfortable accepting the compliments your friends honestly give you.

_____ 9. You're exhausted by trying to get all A's, work 30 hours a week, and be a loving romantic partner at the same. You don't see how so many other people manage to get it all done.

_____ 10. "You're the perfect weight," your father tells you despite your recent gain of twenty pounds over the normal weight for your height.

CHAPTER THREE

▲ Perception: What You See Is What You Get ▲

▲ **I. THE PERCEPTION PROCESS**

   A. Selection

      1. Factors that influence selection

         a. Intense stimuli

         b. Repetitious stimuli

         c. Contract or change in stimulation

         d. Motives

      2. Distortions in selection

         a. Omission

         b. Oversimplification

   B. Organization

      1. Figure–ground organization

      2. Perceptual schema

         a. Physical constructs

         b. Role constructs

         c. Interaction constructs

         d. Psychological constructs

         e. Membership constructs

      3. Effects of organization

         a. Stereotyping

         b. Punctuation

   C. Interpretation—Factors That Influence

      1. Relational satisfaction

      2. Past experience

      3. Assumptions about human behavior

      4. Expectations

      5. Knowledge

      6. Personal mood

II. INFLUENCES ON PERCEPTION

   A. Physiological (Senses, Age, Health, Fatigue, Hunger, Biological Cycles)

▲ KEY TERMS

androgynous	membership constructs
attribution	omission
cultural differences	organization
empathy	oversimplification
figure–ground organization	perception
interaction constructs	perception checking
interpretation	perceptual schema

physical constructs
physiological influences
pillow method
psychological constructs
punctuation
role constructs

selection
self-serving bias
social roles
stereotyping
subcultural differences
sympathy

▲ 3.1 GUARDING AGAINST PERCEPTUAL ERRORS

PURPOSES

1. To help you identify strong positive and negative opinions you have formed about people.
2. To help you recognize some perceptual errors which may have contributed to those strong opinions.

INSTRUCTIONS

1. Identify two people of whom you've formed strong opinions. These opinions can be positive or negative. In either case, describe them.
2. Using the checklist provided, comment on how accurate or inaccurate your perceptions are of each person (see Chapter 3 of *Looking Out/Looking In* for a more detailed description of the checklist factors). Note: Not every factor may apply to each person.
3. Record your conclusions at the end of the exercise.
4. Compare your examples with those of other classmates.

	Example	Person A	Person B
Identify each person. Describe your opinions.	Joni is my wife's good friend. I don't like her; I think she's inconsiderate and selfish and boring. Her voice is shrill and I find her annoying.		
1. We are influenced by what is most obvious.	Because she is my wife's friend, Joni is around a lot, and it seems that I am always noticing her voice or her calls—perhaps I'm looking for them.		
2. We cling to first impressions, even if wrong.	I haven't liked Joni from the beginning. She always used to call right at our dinner time. Even though she doesn't do this any-more, I still remember it and I'm influenced by it.		

	Example	Person A	Person B
3. We tend to assume others are similar to us.			
4. We judge ourselves more charitably than others.	When Joni lost her job, I thought it was Joni's fault because she's so annoying. Of course, when I got laid off a few months later, I complained heavily about the economy and knew being laid off had nothing to do with my performance or personality.		

CONCLUSIONS

Based on the observations above, how accurate or inaccurate are your perceptions of other people?

_____

_____

_____

_____

What might you do in the future to guard against inaccurate perceptions of people?

_____

_____

_____

_____

▲ 3.2 CULTURE AND PERCEPTION

PURPOSES

1. To help you identify the cultural, subcultural, sex, and occupational factors which cause you and another significant person to perceive everyday occurrences differently.
2. To help you minimize conflicts by taking these differences into account.

INSTRUCTIONS

1. Record three differences of opinion you've had with important people in your life.
2. Describe whether these differences of opinion were due to social, occupational, or cultural factors.
3. Explain what you've written to your partner, and record the consequences of your explanation.
4. When you've completed your diary, record your conclusions at the end of this exercise.

OPTION:

Discuss 1–4 above in groups in class, and prepare three examples to deliver to the entire class.

EXAMPLE

Difference of opinion *My roommate and I are always arguing about the number of plants I want to keep in our apartment and out on the balcony. I think the plants give our place a "homey" feeling and really dress up drab walls or hide the fact that we have little furniture. He thinks it makes the place look "junky" and that the plants are a lot of trouble, harbor bugs, and are a pain to care for when I'm not around.*

Factors influencing opinions *There are some subcultural factors at work here; I was raised in a warm climate where plants grew easily and my family always had plants in most rooms of the house; we really had a nice home, and I miss it. Stan was raised in a cold climate, and his family's home was nice, but sparse; he likes everything to look very neat and in its place. Another factor is occupational; I'm a horti-culture major and feel "out of my element" if I don't have some growing things around me. Stan's a computer science major, and he'd rather spend money on new programs for his computer than plant food and potting soil.*

Explanation/consequences *At first Stan started to get defensive when I told him what I was writing about, but when he saw that I did understand his "side" of the issue, he seemed to soften. We talked about it some more, and we agreed to keep plants only in certain rooms of the apartment, and that we would discuss the money each of us spends for our plant/computer interests before we put out the money.*

1. Difference of opinion _____

_____

_____

_____

_____

Factors influencing opinions _____

_____

_____

_____

_____

Explanation/consequences _____

_____

_____

_____

_____

2. Difference of opinion _____

_____

_____

_____

_____

Factors influencing opinions _____

_____

_____

_____

_____

Explanation/consequences _____

_____

_____

_____

_____

3. Difference of opinion _____

_____

_____

_____

_____

   Factors influencing opinions _____

_____

_____

_____

_____

   Explanation/consequences _____

_____

_____

_____

_____

CONCLUSIONS

Based on your observations here, what cultural or societal factors lead to differences of opinions?

_____

_____

_____

What effect does explaining the factors causing your differences have on the outcome of the issue? Are there certain times when it is good to explain cultural and society factors and other times when it might be beneficial to avoid the explanation?

_____

_____

_____

▲ 3.3 EXAMINING YOUR INTERPRETATIONS

PURPOSES

1. To help you identify the interpretations you make about others' behavior in your important interpersonal relationships.
2. To help you recognize the perceptual factors which influence those assumptions.
3. To help you consider the validity of your interpretations.

INTRODUCTION

There are many ways to interpret what another person says or does. For example, you may notice that a new classmate is wearing a cross necklace and imagine that she is a religious person, or you might notice that a friend isn't making much eye contact with you and assume that he is not telling you the truth.

We usually assume that our interpretations are accurate. In fact, these assumptions might be incorrect or quite different from how the other person sees him/herself.

INSTRUCTIONS

1. For the next few days, observe three people and use the spaces below to record your interpretations of each.
2. After completing the information below, share your observations with each person involved and see if your interpretations match the explanations of each subject.

EXAMPLE

Name _____*Stan Morris*_____ context _____*Neighbor and friend*_____

A. Describe an assumption about this person's thoughts or feelings.

I've been thinking that Stan is mad at me, probably because I've been asking so many favors of him lately.

B. Describe at least two items of behavior (things the person has said or done) that lead you to believe your assumption about this person's thoughts or feelings are accurate.

1. *When I asked to borrow his backpacking gear he said yes, but he mentioned several times how much it cost him.*

2. *When I asked him for a ride to school last week when my car was in the shop, he said OK but didn't talk much and drove more quickly than usual.*

C. Give at least two reasons why your assumption about this person's thoughts or feelings may *not* be accurate. (You may ask the person you are observing for help.)

1. *Stan is often a moody person. Even if he is upset, it may not be because of anything I've said or done.*

2. *I'm often hard on myself, taking the blame for anything that goes wrong. Perhaps I'm doing that here, and Stan doesn't mind doing me the favors.*

D. Which of the following factors influenced your perception of this person? Explain how each of these factors affected the accuracy or inaccuracy of your interpretations.

Physiological influences _____

_____

_____

Sex/occupational roles *Perhaps my being a woman has something to do with my self-doubt. I often wonder if I'm being too "forward" in asking a man for favors.*

Cultural/subcultural roles _____

_____

_____

Self-concept *I often view myself as less desirable as a friend than other people I know. I think this leads me to interpret others' reactions as confirmations of my worst fears, whether or not those fears are valid.*

PERSON 1

Name _____ Context _____

A. Describe an assumption you have made about this person's thoughts or feelings.

_____

_____

_____

B. Describe at least two items of behavior (things the person has said or done) that lead you to believe your assumption about this person's thoughts or feelings are accurate.

1. _____

_____

_____

2. _____

_____

_____

C. Give at least two reasons why your assumption about this person's thoughts or feelings may *not* be accurate. (You may ask the person you are observing for help.)

1. _____

_____

_____

2. _____

_____

_____

D. Which of the following factors influence your perception of this person? Explain how each of these factors affected the accuracy or inaccuracy of your interpretations.

Physiological influences _____

_____

_____

Sex/occupational roles _____

_____

_____

Cultural/subcultural roles _____

_____

_____

Self-concept _____

_____

_____

PERSON 2

Name _____ Context _____

A. Describe an assumption you have made about this person's thoughts or feelings.

_____

_____

_____

B. Describe at least two items of behavior (things the person has said or done) that lead you to believe your assumption about this person's thoughts or feelings are accurate.

1. _____

_____

_____

2. _____

_____

_____

C. Give at least two reasons why your assumption about this person's thoughts or feelings may *not* be accurate. (You may ask the person you are observing for help.)

1. _____

_____

_____

2. _____

_____

_____

D. Which of the following factors influenced your perception of this person? Explain how each of these factors affected the accuracy or inaccuracy of your interpretations.

Physiological influences _____

_____

_____

Sex/occupational roles _____

_____

_____

Cultural/subcultural roles _____

_____

_____

Self-concept _____

_____

_____

PERSON 3

Name _____ Context _____

A. Describe an assumption you have made about this person's thoughts or feelings.

_____

_____

_____

B. Describe at least two items of behavior (things the person has said or done) that lead you to believe your assumption about this person's thoughts or feelings are accurate.

1. _____

_____

_____

2. _____

_____

_____

C. Give at least two reasons why your assumption about this person's thoughts or feelings may *not* be accurate. (You may ask the person you are observing for help.)

1. _____

_____

_____

2. _____

_____

_____

D. Which of the following factors influenced your perception of this person? Explain how each of these factors affected the accuracy or inaccuracy of your interpretations.

Physiological influences _____

_____

_____

Sex/occupational roles _____

_____

_____

Cultural/subcultural roles _____

_____

_____

Self-concept _____

_____

_____

▲ 3.4 PERCEPTION CHECKING PRACTICE

PURPOSES

1. To report your observations of another person clearly and accurately.
2. To report at least two interpretations about the meaning of your observations to another person.

INSTRUCTIONS

1. Use the form below to record behavior for each relationship listed.
2. For each example of behavior, record two plausible interpretations.
3. Join with a partner and rehearse how you could share with the person in question each example of behavior and the possible interpretations you have developed. Use the space provided to record your perception checking statement. The statement should include:
    a. The behavior you have observed
    b. Both interpretations
    c. Your request that the recipient of your message help you interpret his/her behavior accurately
4. After the first person in your dyad has completed all the statements below, switch roles so that the other partner follows the same steps.

EXAMPLE

Person	Behavior	Interpretation A	Interpretation B
An instructor (Prof. Smith)	Calls on me at least once each class, even when I don't raise my hand.	Smith is out to get me— wants to make me look like a fool.	Smith wants me to master the course material and thinks challenging me is the best way.

Perception checking statement *Professor Smith, I'm confused about something. I've noticed that you call on me quite often—at least once each class, whether or not I raise my hand. Sometimes I wonder if you're trying to catch me unprepared. On the other hand, sometimes I think you're trying to challenge me by forcing me to keep on my toes. Can you tell me why you call on me so often?*

Name of Family Member	Behavior	Interpretation A	Interpretation B

Perception checking statement _____

_____

_____

_____

Name of Friend	Behavior	Interpretation A	Interpretation B

Perception checking statement _____

_____

_____

_____

Name of Fellow Student or Co-worker	Behavior	Interpretation A	Interpretation B

Perception checking statement _____

_____

_____

_____

▲ 3.5 APPLYING PERCEPTION CHECKING

PURPOSE

To prepare and deliver effective perception checking statements.

INSTRUCTIONS

1. Choose two people with whom you have relational concerns. Give careful consideration to the partners you choose, choose concerns that are real and important, and allow yourself enough time to discuss your concerns with each partner.
2. Identify the concern, its importance to you, and consider the best time and place to approach each person.
3. Prepare perception checking statements to deliver to each person.
4. Deliver your perception statements, discussing with each person your understanding of his/her behavior and the accuracy or inaccuracy of your perceptions.

PARTNER 1

PART ONE: DESCRIBE YOUR CONCERN

Partner's name _____

A. Describe your primary concern. _____

_____

_____

B. Why is it important to you to clarify this matter? _____

_____

_____

C. When and where is the best time to talk with this person? _____

_____

_____

PART TWO: PREPARING YOUR PERCEPTION CHECKING STATEMENT

A. Describe your observations of the other person's behavior. _____

_____

_____

B. Write one interpretation which you believe could explain the behaviors you have observed.

_____

_____

_____

C. Now write a second interpretation which is distinctly different from your previous one and which you believe could also explain the behavior you have observed.

_____

_____

_____

PART THREE: SHARING YOUR PERCEPTION CHECKING STATEMENT

Meet with your partner and (1) share your description of this person's behavior by describing the sense data you have observed, (2) explain both of your interpretations of the sense data, and (3) ask your partner to react to the interpretations you have shared.

Describe the outcome of your conversation with your partner. _____

_____

_____

_____

_____

PARTNER 2

PART ONE: DESCRIBE YOUR CONCERN

Partner's name _____

A. Describe your primary concern. _____

_____

_____

B. Why is it important to you to clarify this matter? _____

_____

_____

C. When and where is the best time to talk with this person? _____

_____

_____

PART TWO: PREPARING YOUR PERCEPTION CHECKING STATEMENT

A. Describe your observations of the other person's behavior. _____

_____

_____

B. Write one interpretation which you believe could explain the behaviors you have observed.

_____

_____

_____

C. Now write a second interpretation which is distinctly different from your previous one and which you believe could also explain the behavior you have observed.

_____

_____

_____

PART THREE: SHARING YOUR PERCEPTION CHECKING STATEMENT

Meet with your partner and (1) share your description of this person's behavior by describing the sense data you have observed, (2) explain both of your interpretations of the sense data, and (3) ask your partner to react to the interpretations you have shared.

Describe the outcome of your conversation with your partner. _____

_____

_____

_____

_____

SUMMARY

1. How accurate were your interpretations in the two situations above?

    _____

    _____

    _____

2. Based on your experiences in this exercise, in what circumstances are your interpretations accurate? When are they likely to be inaccurate? Consider the people involved, the topic of communication, and your personal moods and thoughts.

    _____

    _____

    _____

    _____

3. How did your partners react when you communicated by using perception checking? How did these reactions differ from the reactions you get when you jump to conclusions instead of using perception checking?

    _____

    _____

    _____

4. Based on your experience in this exercise, when and how can you use perception checking in your everyday communication? With whom? In what situations? What difference will using perception checking make in your interpersonal relationships?

    _____

    _____

    _____

    _____

    _____

▲ 3.6 PERCEPTION CHECKING DIARY

PURPOSES

1. To help you identify the opportunities to use perception checking.
2. To help you learn the degree to which you use perception checking.
3. To help you discover the consequences of using and not using perception checking.
4. To help you distinguish between facts and inferences.

INSTRUCTIONS

1. For the next several days, record three situations in which it might be useful to use perception checking.
2. Describe your perception of the situation, including your interpretations.
3. Write a perception checking statement which allows you to check out your interpretations (also helps you recognize your tendency to make inferences from the facts presented). Include in your statement: (a) a description of the situation, (b) your interpretation(s) of the situation, including feelings if appropriate, and (c) a request of the other for confirmation of your interpretation(s).
4. Record the consequences of sharing the perception checking statement.
5. Record a situation similar to the first three in which you decided not to use a perception checking statement. Record the consequences of not making a perception checking statement. Give your reasons for deciding against perception checking.
6. After concluding your diary, summarize your discoveries in the spaces provided.

EXAMPLE

Situation *I went to a party with Rob at his friend's place. Rob knew almost everyone there, and I didn't know anyone.*

Your perception of the situation *I thought Rob ignored me all night long and flirted with every woman at the party.*

Perception checking statement
(a) *"When you spent all that time talking to other women and leaving me alone,*
(b) *I thought you were bored with me and flirting with them. I felt hurt and alone.*
(c) *Were you bored with me or what?"*

Consequences *Rob got defensive at first, partly due to my accusing tone of voice, I think. Then we talked about my need for some support in unfamiliar situations and my need to be reassured that he cares about me.*

1. Situation _____

   _____

   _____

Your perception of the situation _____

_____

_____

_____

Perception checking statement _____

(a) _____

(b) _____

(c) _____

Consequences _____

_____

_____

_____

_____

2. Situation _____

_____

_____

Your perception of the situation _____

_____

_____

_____

Perception checking statement _____

(a) _____

(b) _____

(c) _____

Consequences _____

_____

_____

_____

_____

3. Situation _____

_____

_____

Your perception of the situation _____

_____

_____

Perception checking statement _____

(a) _____

(b) _____

(c) _____

Consequences _____

_____

_____

_____

4. Situation in which I decided not to perception check _____

_____

_____

_____

_____

My perception of the situation _____

_____

_____

_____

Reasons why I decided not to perception check _____

_____

_____

_____

Consequences _____

_____

_____

CONCLUSIONS

Based on your observations, how frequently do you check your perceptions when the opportunity arises?

_____

_____

_____

_____

_____

When in the future might you improve your relationships by making more perception checking statement(s)?

_____

_____

_____

_____

_____

_____

▲ 3.7 ORAL SKILL—PERCEPTION CHECKING

PURPOSE

To create effective perception checking statements.

INSTRUCTIONS

OPTION A:

Practice writing perception checking statements for items 1–10 below.

OPTION B:

1. Join with a partner to create a dyad. Label one person A and the other B.
2. Both A and B should write perception checking statements for items 1–10 below.
3. A then delivers items 1–5 to B orally. B should use Evaluation Form 3.9 to rate A's responses for these items.
4. B delivers items 6–10 orally to A. A should use Evaluation Form 3.9 to rate B's responses for these items.

OPTION C:

Practice items 1–10 below orally with a partner. Deliver your best perception check in class while your instructor evaluates you.

EXAMPLE

Yesterday you saw your friend walking on the beach engaged in what looked to you like an intense conversation with your recent date, Chris.

Perception checking statement *When I saw you yesterday walking on the beach with Chris, I didn't know what to make of it. I thought you might be talking about that class you're taking together, but I also wondered whether you're interested in dating Chris. Are you interested in Chris as a friend, or as a date?*

1. During last week's exam you thought you saw your friend Jim, who sits next to you in class, looking at your paper.

_____

_____

_____

_____

2. Ever since the school year began, your parents have made a point of asking how you are doing several times each month. They have just asked again.

_____

_____

_____

3. Your friend Jake was driving you home from a party last night when he began to weave the car between lanes on the highway. You were uncomfortable, but didn't say anything then. Now it is the next morning and Jake shows up to take you to a class. You have decided to bring up the incident.

_____

_____

_____

4. Last month you had a long talk with your friend Betty about her troubled engagement. Now you run into her in the shopping mall, and she talks for ten minutes about what she is doing without mentioning her fiancé.

_____

_____

_____

5. You return home at night to find your roommate, Tom, reading on the couch. When you walk into the room and greet Tom, he grunts and turns his face away from you and keeps reading.

_____

_____

_____

6. Last week your instructor, Dr. Green, returned your exam with a low grade and the comment "This kind of work paints a bleak picture for the future." You have approached him to discuss the remark.

_____

_____

_____

7. In one of your regular long distance phone conversations you ask your favorite cousin, Mike, about the state of his up-and-down romantic life. He sighs and says, "Oh, it's OK, I guess."

_____

_____

_____

8. Your girl/boyfriend (or spouse) announces that s/he plans to spend next Friday night with friends from work. You usually spend Friday nights alone together.

_____

_____

_____

9. Last week your supervisor at work, Ms. White, gave you a big assignment. Three times since then she has asked you whether you're having any trouble with it.

_____

_____

_____

10. Last weekend your next-door neighbor, Steve, raked a big pile of leaves near your property line, promising to clean them up after work on Monday. It's Wednesday, and the wind is blowing the leaves into your yard.

_____

_____

_____

11. One of your classmates sits by you every day in class and runs after you to walk across campus; now he has started calling you at home every evening. He now suggests that you do some things on the weekend together.

_____

_____

_____

12. You've noticed one of your office mates looking over at you a number of times during the past few days. At first she looked away quickly, but now she smiles every time you look up and catch her looking at you. You've been under a lot of pressure at work lately and have been extremely busy. You can't understand why she keeps looking at you. You've decided to ask.

_____

_____

_____

13. It seems that every time you have been leaving your house lately, your roommate runs after you, asking for a ride somewhere. Your roommate has a car, but you haven't seen it lately. You are in a hurry now, and your roommate has just asked for another ride.

_____

_____

_____

▲ 3.8 CHECKLIST FOR ORAL SKILL—PERCEPTION CHECKING

PURPOSE

To create effective perception checking statements.

INSTRUCTIONS

1. Deliver perception checking statements to one another according to the instructions for perception checking in *3.7 Oral Skill—Perception Checking* or a situation your instructor presents.
2. Use the criteria below to be evaluated.

CHECKLIST

5 = superior   4 = excellent   3 = good   2 = fair   1 = poor

Reports at least one behavior that describes what the person has said or done.   _____

States two interpretations that are distinctly different, equally probable, and are based on the reported behavior.   _____

Makes an objective and open-ended request for feedback on how to interpret the reported behavior.   _____

Consistently uses language that accepts responsibility for the interpretations made.   _____

Consistently uses nonthreatening, nondefensive voice and appropriate eye contact.   _____

                                                                           Total   _____

▲ 3.9 SHIFTING PERSPECTIVES (PILLOW METHOD)

PURPOSES

1. To help you understand how others view an interpersonal issue.
2. To help you recognize the merits and drawbacks of each person's perspective.
3. To help you recognize how an interpersonal issue may not be as important as it first seems.

INSTRUCTIONS

1. Select one disagreement or other issue which is now affecting an interpersonal relationship.
2. Record enough background information for an outsider to understand the issue. Who is involved? How long has the disagreement been going on? What are the basic issues involved?
3. Describe the issue from each of the four positions listed below.
4. Record your conclusions at the end of this exercise.

OPTION:

With a partner, role-play your situation orally, using 3.10 *Checklist for Oral Skill—Pillow Method.*

Background Information

_____

_____

_____

_____

_____

_____

Position 1: Explain how you are right and the other person is wrong.

_____

_____

_____

_____

_____

_____

_____

Position 2: Explain how the other person's position is correct, or at least understandable.

_____

_____

_____

_____

_____

_____

Position 3: Show that there are both correct (or understandable) and mistaken (or unreasonable) parts of both positions.

_____

_____

_____

_____

_____

_____

Position 4: Describe at least two ways in which the elements developed in positions 1–3 might affect your relationship. Describe at least one way in which the issue might be seen as *less* important than it was originally, and describe at least one way in which the issue might be seen as *more* important than it was originally.

_____

_____

_____

_____

_____

_____

CONCLUSION

Explain how there is some truth in each of the preceding positions. Also explain how viewing the issue from each of the preceding positions has changed your perception of the issue, and how it may change your behavior in the future. Explain how this issue and your understanding of it affect your relationship.

_____

_____

_____

_____

_____

_____

▲ 3.10 CHECKLIST FOR ORAL SKILL—PILLOW METHOD

PURPOSE

To use the Pillow Method to illustrate understanding of at least two perspectives on a given issue.

INSTRUCTIONS

Using *3.9 Shifting Perspectives (Pillow Method)* as a guide, prepare to deliver to the class (or videotape/instructor) your version of your perspective on an issue and that of your partner. Get your real-life partner to listen in and correct you if you have misunderstood his or her position, or ask a classmate to role-play your partner, interrupting you if s/he thinks another aspect of the issue has been neglected. Use perception checking, as necessary, to clarify perceptions with your partner.

CHECKLIST

5 = superior   4 = excellent   3 = good   2 = fair   1 = poor

Engages in appropriate nonverbal behavior   _____
    —looks at partner
    —speaks in nondefensive tone
    —faces partner

Presents relevant background information   _____

Explains Position 1 (I'm right; other person is wrong)   _____

Explains Position 2 (partner is correct/understandable)   _____

Explains Position 3 (both positions are correct/mistaken—even partly)   _____

Explains Position 4 (effects on relationship)   _____

Uses perception checking as necessary   _____

Presents conclusion   _____

                                        Total   _____

▲ 3.11 RECOGNIZING PERCEPTION-CHECKING ELEMENTS

PURPOSE

To practice recognizing elements of perception-checking statements.

INSTRUCTIONS

1. Study the statements below to discover whether all of the elements of perception-checking are present or if there are any missing.
2. Record your answer on the line in front of the statement.
3. Check your answers in the back of this manual on page 281.

For each of the following statements, identify which element of the perception-checking statement is missing. Place the letter of the most accurate evaluation of the statement on the line before the statement.

    a.   This statement doesn't describe behavior.
    b.   This statement doesn't give two distinctly different interpretations.
    c.   This statement neglects to request clarification of the perception.
    d.   There is nothing missing from this perception-checking statement.

_____   1.   "Why did you send me those flowers? Is this a special occasion or what?"

_____   2.   "When you went straight to bed when you came home, I thought you were sick. Are you all right?"

_____   3.   "You must be either really excited about your grades or anxious to talk about something important. What's going on?"

_____   4.   "When you ran out smiling, I figured you were glad to see me and ready to go, or maybe you were having such a good time here you wanted to stay longer."

_____   5.   "I thought you were angry with me when you didn't come over this afternoon like you'd said you would. But then I thought maybe something came up at work. What is it?"

_____   6.   "When you told me you expected to get an outline with my report, I thought you were trying to trick me into doing more work, or maybe you didn't realize that wasn't part of my job."

_____   7.   "When you told everyone my parents own the company, you must have been indicating I was hired here only because of them. Is that what you think?"

_____   8.   "When you passed the ball to me, I thought you wanted me to shoot. Did you?"

_____   9.   "Why is it that you're so pleased with yourself? Did you win the lottery or accomplish something great? What's up?"

_____   10.   "Dad, when you told my friend Art what a great athlete you think I am, I thought you were either really proud of me and wanted to brag a little, or maybe you wanted to see what Art and I had in common by the way he responded. What were you up to?"

CHAPTER FOUR

▲ Emotions ▲

▲ **I. COMPONENTS OF EMOTIONS**
  A. Physiological Changes
  B. Nonverbal Reactions
  C. Cognitive Interpretations

II. TYPES OF EMOTIONS
  A. Primary and Mixed
  B. Intense and Mild

III. INFLUENCES ON EMOTIONAL EXPRESSION
  A. Culture
  B. Gender
  C. Social Conventions
  D. Social Roles
  E. Inability to Recognize Emotions
  F. Fear of Self-Disclosure

IV. GUIDELINES FOR EXPRESSING EMOTIONS
  A. Recognize Feelings
  B. Choose the Best Language
  C. Share Mixed Feelings
  D. Recognize Difference Between Feeling and Acting
  E. Accept Responsibility for Your Feelings
  F. Choose the Best Time and Place to Express Your Feelings

G. **Express Your Feelings Clearly**
   1. Summarize in a few words/avoid excessive length
   2. Avoid overqualification or downplaying
   3. Avoid "coded" feelings
   4. Focus on a specific set of circumstances

V. **MANAGING DIFFICULT EMOTIONS**
   A. **Facilitative and Debilitative Emotions**
      1. Intensity
      2. Duration
   B. **Thoughts Can Cause Feelings**
   C. **Irrational Thinking and Debilitative Emotions**
      1. Fallacy of perfection
      2. Fallacy of approval
      3. Fallacy of shoulds
      4. Fallacy of overgeneralization
         a. Limited amount of evidence
         b. Exaggerated shortcomings
         c. Abuse of the verb "to be"
      5. Fallacy of causation
         a. You cause emotions/pain for others
         b. Others cause your emotions
      6. Fallacy of helplessness
      7. Fallacy of catastrophic expectations
   D. **Minimizing Debilitative Emotions**
      1. Monitor your emotional reactions
      2. Note the activating event
      3. Record your self-talk
      4. Dispute your irrational beliefs

▲ KEY TERMS

activating event
cognitive interpretations
debilitative emotions
downplaying
duration
emotional counterfeits
emotions
facilitative emotions
fallacy of approval
fallacy of catastrophic expectations
fallacy of causation
fallacy of helplessness
fallacy of overgeneralization

fallacy of perfection
fallacy of shoulds
intensity
irrational fallacies
mixed emotions
nonverbal reactions
overqualifying
physiological changes
Plutchik's "emotion wheel"
primary emotions
proprioceptive stimuli
rational–emotive therapy
self-talk

▲ 4.1 THE COMPONENTS OF EMOTION

PURPOSE

To help you identify the components of emotion.

INSTRUCTIONS

Read each of the situations described below and describe how the emotions you would experience might manifest themselves in each of the components listed.

Incident	Emotion(s)	Physiological Changes	Nonverbal Reactions	Cognitive Interpretation (Thoughts)
Example You've been assigned to deliver an oral presentation in one of your classes. It's now time to give your speech.	nervousness	pounding heart, churning stomach	quivery voice, slightly trembling hands	"I hope I don't make a fool of myself."
1. You're out on the town with friends for the evening. A companion asks you to dance.				
2. You're trying to study when a friend drops by, prepared to chat.				
3. You're telling a joke or story. Just as you reach the punch line, you notice your listener stifle a yawn.				
4. At the beginning of class, one of your professors says, "I'd like to talk to you in my office after the lecture."				

Incident	Emotion(s)	Physiological Changes	Nonverbal Reactions	Cognitive Interpretation (Thoughts)
5. An attractive friend whom you'd like to know better approaches you after an absence and gives you a hug, saying, "It's great to see you."				
6. You're discussing politics with a friend, who says, "I don't see how you can believe that!"				
7. A friend or relative has forgotten your birthday. S/he now apologizes.				
8. You overhear two preschool children pointing at you and saying, "Look at that silly!"				
9. Your romantic partner proposes marriage in front of friends. You're not ready.				
10. You are going in to your boss's office for your annual appraisal interview.				

▲ 4.2 FIND THE FEELINGS

PURPOSES

1. To help you distinguish true feeling statements from counterfeit expressions of emotion.
2. To increase your ability to express your feelings clearly.

INSTRUCTIONS

1. Identify any true feeling statements below.
2. Rewrite statements which do not clearly or accurately express the speaker's feelings. (Hint: Statements which could be prefaced with "I think" are not expressions of emotions. If the statements could be preceded by "I am," there is a good likelihood that they express feelings.)
3. Check your answers in the back of this manual on page 281.

EXAMPLE

That's the most disgusting thing I've ever heard!
Analysis *This isn't a satisfactory statement, since the speaker isn't clearly claiming that he or she is disgusted.*

1. That was a great evening!

   Analysis _____

   _____

   _____

2. You're being awfully sensitive about that.

   Analysis _____

   _____

   _____

3. I can't figure out how to approach him.

   Analysis _____

   _____

   _____

4. I'm confused about what you want from me.

   Analysis _____

   _____

   _____

5. I love the way you've been so helpful.

   Analysis _____

   _____

   _____

6. I feel as if you're trying to hurt me.

   Analysis _____

   _____

   _____

7. It's hopeless!

   Analysis _____

   _____

   _____

8. I don't know how to tell you this . . .

   Analysis _____

   _____

   _____

9. What's bothering you?

   Analysis _____

   _____

   _____

10. I feel like the rug's been pulled out from under me.

   Analysis _____

   _____

   _____

▲ 4.3 DISTINGUISHING AND LABELING EMOTIONS

PURPOSES

1. To help you put labels on the feelings you have.
2. To describe your probable behavior when feeling a specific emotion.
3. To describe how the emotions you've labeled are facilitative or debilitative.

INSTRUCTIONS

1. In the second column below, describe your reaction to each of the situations listed. Label the emotions you might have and your probable behavior.
2. Describe in the third column how each emotion you've listed (and the behavior accompanying it) might be facilitative or debilitative for you.
3. Complete the questions at the end of the exercise.

Situation	Label Your Emotions and Behavior	Describe Facilitative/Debilitative Aspects of Your Emotions
Example You spend many hours studying for a test. The night before it's to be given, a friend asks to see your notes, claiming that you're really on top of the material.	Insulted—I say "I feel uncomfortable giving you information I've spent hours preparing."	*Facilitative*—without "caving in" and giving away notes *or* getting really angry and yelling, this expression of my feeling is honest and helps me feel good about myself. *Debilitative*—I may spend too much time worrying about the effects of my words. I may worry about losing my friend's friendship; I might really lose the friendship. Maybe my friend will yell back at me or tell others bad things about me.
1. Several of your letters to a friend in another city have gone unanswered. Finally you phone, and the friend assures you that nothing is wrong.		
2. A friend has been avoiding you lately and acting in an aloof manner.		

Situation	Label Your Emotions and Behavior	Describe Facilitative/Debilitative Aspects of Your Emotions
3. A friend shows you a painting s/he has done and asks your opinion. You don't like it at all.		
4. You notice an attractive person across the room. That person catches you glancing at him/her.		
5. You've been preoccupied with some personal matters. A relative or friend says you're being silly for worrying so much.		
6. A friend continually "borrows" money from you and "forgets" to pay it back.		
7. While reviewing an exam in class, your instructor praises one of your answers.		

Situation	Label Your Emotions and Behavior	Describe Facilitative/Debilitative Aspects of Your Emotions
8. You have just told a friend that you're going on a healthy diet. That morning you go out to breakfast together and you order a large stack of pancakes. Your friend teases you.		
9. You and a friend have been planning to spend a weekend day together. On Friday night, you realize you'd rather have the time to yourself. Just then the friend calls.		

CONCLUSIONS

Compare the situations in this exercise to situations in your own life. How easily do you label your emotions? Are you happy with your behavior in these situations? Describe specific instances and why you are pleased or unpleased with your emotional behavior.

_____

_____

_____

_____

Based on your facilitative and debilitative descriptions above, comment on your ability to clarify the facilitative and debilitative aspects of your emotions. Give specific examples.

_____

_____

_____

_____

▲ 4.4 STATING EMOTIONS EFFECTIVELY

PURPOSE

To help you express the emotions you experience clearly and appropriately.

INSTRUCTIONS

1. Identify what's ineffective or unclear about each of the following feeling statements.
2. Rewrite the feeling statements making them more effective. Use the following guidelines for sharing feelings:
   Recognize feelings
   Choose the best language
   Share mixed feelings
   Differentiate between feeling and acting
   Accept responsibility for your feelings
   Choose the best time and place to express
   Express your feelings clearly

Feeling Statement	Identify Ineffective/Unclear Elements/Rewrite Statement
Example When you complimented me in front of everyone at the party, I was really embarrassed.	I didn't express the mixed emotions I was feeling. I could have expressed this better by saying, "When you complimented me at the party, I was glad you were proud of me, but I was embarrassed that you did it in front of so many people."
1. You make me so mad.	
2. I can't believe you act like that— I don't want to see you anymore.	
3. I don't care if you are rushed. We have to settle this now.	

Feeling Statement	Identify Ineffective/Unclear Elements/Rewrite Statement
4. I was a little ticked off when you didn't show up.	
5. You're always criticizing me.	
6. Sure would be nice if people expressed appreciation.	
7. You jerk—you forgot to put gas in the car.	
8. It's about time you paid up.	
9. You're the best!	
10. Thanks for everything!	
11. I guess I'm a little attracted to him.	
12. She sends me into outer space.	

▲ 4.5 RECOGNIZING YOUR EMOTIONS

PURPOSE

To help you identify the emotions you experience, how you deal with them, and consequences of your emotional style.

INSTRUCTIONS

1. Observe your thoughts, feelings, and behaviors for several days. Fill in the appropriate spaces below.
2. After completing the form, answer the questions that follow it.

Emotion(s)	Who Is Involved? In What Circumstances?	How Did You Recognize Emotion?	What Did You Do? (verbal and nonverbal behavior)	Consequences of Your Action (for yourself and for others)
Example embarrassment, anger	My friend J. kidded me about my repeated vows to start exercising and pointed out that I was looking "like a wimp." This was done in front of other friends.	I felt myself blush, thought to myself, "Now they're all thinking what a lazy, ugly slug I am!"	I pretended to laugh the matter off. (I don't think my act was very convincing.)	I was mad at myself for deserving the criticism (it was true), and for not saying something to my friend. Also, I feel a bit self-conscious around the friends who were there.
1.				
2.				
3.				
4.				
5.				

CONCLUSIONS

1. What emotions do you experience most commonly? In what circumstances, and with what people?

   _____

   _____

   _____

   _____

   _____

2. How do you recognize your emotions?

   _____

   _____

   _____

   _____

   _____

3. In what ways do you deal with your emotions? What are the consequences—for you and others—of this style?

   _____

   _____

   _____

   _____

   _____

4. Are there any ways in which you would like to change your emotion-related communication?

   _____

   _____

   _____

   _____

   _____

▲ 4.7 DISPUTING IRRATIONAL THOUGHTS

PURPOSE

To help you minimize debilitative emotions by eliminating irrational thinking.

INSTRUCTIONS

1. Use the chart below to record incidents in which you experience communication-related debilitative emotions. The incidents needn't involve overwhelming feelings: mildly debilitative emotions are appropriate for consideration as well.
2. For each incident (activating event), record the self-talk that leads to the emotion you experienced.
3. If the self-talk you've identified is based on any of the irrational fallacies described in *Looking Out/Looking In*, identify them.
4. In each case where irrational thinking exists, dispute the irrational fallacies and provide an alternative, more rational interpretation of the event.
5. Record your conclusions in the section at the end of this exercise.

Activating Event	Self-Talk	Based on Any Irrational Fallacies?	Emotion(s)	Dispute Irrational Thinking and Provide Alternative Interpretation
Example getting ready for job interview	"The employer will probably ask me a question I can't answer. I'll probably blow the interview. I'll never get a good job—it's hopeless!"	catastrophic failure overgeneralization helplessness	apprehension	There's certainly a *chance* that I'll blow the interview, but there's at least as good a chance that I'll do all right. I'm going overboard when I tell myself that there's no hope. The smartest idea is to do my best and not create a self-fulfilling prophecy of failing.
1.				
2.				
3.				
4.				
5.				

CONCLUSIONS

1. What are the situations in which you often experience debilitative emotions?

_____

_____

_____

_____

2. What irrational beliefs do you subscribe to most often?

_____

_____

_____

_____

3. How can you think more rationally to reduce the number and intensity of irrational emotions? (Give specific examples related to the activating events you have described in this exercise.)

_____

_____

_____

_____

_____

_____

_____

_____

▲ 4.8 EXPRESSING FACILITATIVE EMOTIONS

PURPOSE

To express the facilitative emotions you experience clearly and appropriately by using the guidelines for sharing feelings.

INSTRUCTIONS

1. List events from your recent life in which you should have expressed or did express your emotions.
2. Describe your thoughts at the time.
3. Express this feeling to another. (Write out how you did express the feeling or how you should have expressed it.)
4. Analyze the clarity and appropriateness of your expression of feeling. Propose alternative expressions of emotion according to the following guidelines for sharing feelings:
   Recognize feelings
   Choose the best language
   Share mixed feelings
   Differentiate between feeling and acting
   Accept responsibility for your feelings
   Choose the best time and place to express
   Express your feelings clearly

OPTION:

Role-play two of the events you've described with a partner in class. Do an oral skill check; explain the event to your partner, describe your thoughts, and then express your feelings as if you were "really there." Analyze the clarity and appropriateness of your chosen expression of emotion for your partner. Use 4.9 *Checklist for Oral Skill—Expressing Facilitative Emotions.*

Event	Thoughts (Self-Talk)	Expression of Feeling	Clarity/Appropriateness (or Alternatives)
Example Chris, my roommate, failed to clean the kitchen after eating.	I want the kitchen cleaned. It is Chris's responsibility to clean up after himself. We agreed we'd each clean up our own dishes. I need to say something to Chris.	"Chris, I'm worried you'll forget to clean up the kitchen—what's happening?"	I think I chose the best *time and place*—immediately—and I accepted *responsibility* for my feelings. I might have chosen *better language* by saying, "I'm upset that you didn't clean up the kitchen tonight as we'd agreed."
1.			
2.			
3.			
4.			
5.			

▲ 4.9 CHECKLIST FOR ORAL SKILL— EXPRESSING FACILITATIVE EMOTIONS

Choose two situations you described in 4.8 and role-play them with a partner, either

  a. (if you were satisfied with your expression) as you did in real life,

or

  b. (if you were unsatisfied) as you would like to, using the guidelines for expressing emotions.

Express two emotions described in 4.8 to your partner. You will be evaluated on your expression of emotion and how it fits the guidelines for sharing emotions. Then you evaluate your partner according to the skill check.

Use the following scale to rate your partner on each expression of emotion:

5 = superior   4 = excellent   3 = good   2 = fair   1 = poor

	Emotion 1	Emotion 2
Chooses the best time and place to express feelings	_____	_____
Chooses the best language to express feelings	_____	_____
Shares mixed feelings as appropriate	_____	_____
Distinguishes between feeling and acting as appropriate	_____	_____
Accepts responsibility for own feelings	_____	_____
Expresses feelings clearly	_____	_____
—summarizes; avoids excessive length —avoids overqualification/downplaying —avoids "coded" feelings —focuses on specific circumstances		
Total	_____	_____

▲ 4.10 IDENTIFYING IRRATIONAL FALLACIES

PURPOSE

To give you practice in identifying irrational fallacies that may lead to debilitative emotions.

INSTRUCTIONS

1. Match the letter of the irrational fallacy with its description of self-talk found below.
2. Check your answers in the back of this manual on p. 282.

   a. perfection
   b. approval
   c. shoulds
   d. overgeneralization
   e. causation
   f. helplessness
   g. catastrophic expectations

_____ 1. "If only I didn't put my foot in my mouth when I ask someone out."

_____ 2. "I just can't initiate conversations—that's all there is to it."

_____ 3. "He shouldn't be off with his friends on Friday night."

_____ 4. "If she doesn't like this shirt, I'll be so upset."

_____ 5. "There was a major fire the last time we left; there will probably be an earthquake this time."

_____ 6. "He's never romantic."

_____ 7. "She's a cold fish; I'm lucky if I get a kiss."

_____ 8. "You ought to drink less."

_____ 9. "You're going to die going to Mexico at spring break."

_____ 10. "I've had a class in interpersonal communication; I can't believe I insulted her just now."

_____ 11. "Shaw makes me so mad with all his great grades."

_____ 12. "She'll be devastated if I break up with her."

_____ 13. "It's not even worth trying to reach him."

_____ 14. "I hope they don't notice how much weight I've gained."

CHAPTER FIVE

▲ Language: Barrier and Bridge ▲

▲ **I. THE NATURE OF LANGUAGE**

    A. Language Is Symbolic

    B. Language Is Subjective

    C. Language Is Rule-Governed
       1. Syntactic: Structure
       2. Semantic
       3. Regulative/pragmatic

  II. THE VERBAL LEVEL: WORDS AND MEANINGS

    A. Distinguish Facts from Inferences

    B. Explain Relative words

    C. Use Euphemisms Sparingly

    D. Use Emotive Words with Caution

    E. Beware of Equivocal Language

    F. Beware of Static Evaluation

    G. Choose the Proper Level of Abstraction
       1. High abstraction advantages
          a. Shorthand
          b. Avoid confusion
       2. High abstraction problems
          a. Stereotyping
          b. Confusing others
          c. Lack of relational clarity
          d. Confuse yourself
       3. Avoiding high-level abstractions with behavioral descriptions
          a. Who is involved?
          b. In what circumstances?
          c. What behaviors are involved?

III. THE INTERPERSONAL LEVEL: LANGUAGE AND RELATIONSHIPS

A. The Language of Responsibility
1. "I" language
   a. Describes behavior
   b. Describes feelings
   c. Describes consequences
2. Advantages of "I" language
   a. Defense reducing
   b. More honest
   c. More complete
3. Problems with "I" language
   a. Anger interferes
   b. Other still gets defensive
   c. Sounds artificial

B. Language and Power
1. Powerful and powerless speech
2. The balance of power in relationships
   a. Complementary communication
   b. Symmetrical communication

IV. THE SOCIETAL LEVEL: LANGUAGE AND COMMUNICATION SYSTEMS

A. Language and Culture
1. Verbal communication styles
   a. Low context/high context (level of directness)
   b. Elaborate/succinct
   c. Formal/informal
2. Language and world view
   a. Linguistic determinism
   b. Sapir-Whorf hypothesis
   c. Linguistic relativism

B. Gender and Language
1. Content
2. Reasons for communicating
3. Conversational style
4. Non-gender variables
5. Sex roles—social orientation

▲ KEY TERMS

abstraction ladder	equivocal language
abstractions	euphemisms
behavioral descriptions	facts
complementary communication	hedges
disclaimers	hesitations
elaborate	high-context culture
emotive language	"I" language

inferences
intensifiers
language of power
language of responsibility
linguistic determinism
linguistic relativism
low-context culture
polite forms
regulative rules
relative words

Sapir-Whorf hypothesis
semantic rules
sex roles
static evaluation
stereotyping
succinct
symmetrical communication
syntactic rules
tag questions
"you" language

NAME _____

▲ 5.1 FACTS AND INFERENCES

PURPOSES

1. To recognize the inferences contained in statements presented as facts in your language and that of your friends.
2. To apply the skill of perception checking learned in Chapter 3 to clarify the inferences you make.

INSTRUCTIONS

1. Consider your school, work, and personal lives during the past few months. From situations that you remember, write down five statements that you made about someone, to someone—or about something that was general and might have many interpretations.
2. Write down at least three inferences you and/or others may have made from your statement.
3. Write the *facts* of the case or situation as they actually occurred.
4. Deliver a perception checking statement to the person involved *or* write a *revised* statement making clear to yourself or someone you are talking to *both* the facts and inferences in the situation.

Situation and What I Said to Myself or Others	Inferences	Facts	Perception Checking
Example I've been feeling really hassled at the office, and I've been thinking my supervisor has a lot to do with it. Last night I found myself muttering under my breath, "You're on me all the time about something or other."	You're trying to make me quit. You want to make me angry. You think I have nothing better to do in the evening than work on reports. You're too lazy to do the reports yourself. You think I'm a sloppy worker. You're trying to force a confrontation with me.	Jim, my supervisor, came into the office the last four evenings at 4:30 and gave me unfinished reports to redo by the next morning.	Jim, when you gave me unfinished reports to do by the next morning each of the last four evenings, I thought you were telling me I was a sloppy worker or were just trying to make me angry. Just why have you given me reports the last four nights?
1.			
2.			

Situation and What I Said to Myself or Others	Inferences	Facts	Perception Checking
3.			
4.			
5.			

▲ 5.2 LABEL THE LANGUAGE

PURPOSE

To help you recognize and change the language described in Chapter 5 of *Looking Out/Looking In*.

INSTRUCTIONS

1. Label the language contained in each of the sentences below as relative language, emotive terms, or equivocal language.
2. Rewrite each sentence in more precise language.
3. Write examples of each variety of language in the space provided.

EXAMPLE

I'm trying to diet, so give me a **small piece of cake.** _____
Language *Relative language* _____
Revised statement *I'm trying to diet, so give me a piece of cake about half the size of yours.* _____

1. I want to talk about **our relationship.**

   Language _____

   Revised statement _____

   _____

2. I'd like you to meet my **roommate** [of opposite sex].

   Language _____

   Revised statement _____

   _____

3. Helen is a **troublemaker**.

   Language _____

   Revised statement _____

   _____

4. Our candidate is trying to bring about a more **peaceful** world.

   Language _____

   Revised statement _____

   _____

5. We've known each other for a **long time**.

   Language _____

   Revised statement _____

   _____

6. Your essay should be **brief**.

   Language _____

   Revised statement _____

   _____

7. She's a very **mature** child for her age.

   Language _____

   Revised statement _____

   _____

8. Your contribution will help make government **more responsible to the people**.

   Language _____

   Revised statement _____

   _____

9. I don't understand **women** (or **men**)!

   Language _____

   Revised statement _____

   _____

10. He's a real **pest**.

   Language _____

   Revised statement _____

   _____

11. Stanley is an **ethical** person.

   Language _____

   Revised statement _____

   _____

12. We need to make some **changes** around here.

   Language _____

   Revised statement _____

   _____

13. I need **room to breathe**.

   Language _____

   Revised statement _____

   _____

14. Let's get her **something really nice**.

   Language _____

   Revised statement _____

Now write your own examples of each type of language, and revise the statements to illustrate alternative language.

1. Equivocal language _____

   _____

   Revised: _____

2. Relative language _____

   _____

   Revised: _____

3. Emotive language _____

   _____

   Revised: _____

▲ 5.3 CHECK YOUR ABSTRACTIONS

PURPOSES

1. To help you identify ways in which you can use overly abstract language.
2. To help you clarify your use of abstract language.
3. To demonstrate the many ways in which overly abstract language can be used.

INSTRUCTIONS

1. Quickly write down your response to each of the incomplete sentences below. Before proceeding further, compare your responses with those of other people
2. After comparing your responses to the incomplete sentences, reduce the subject of each sentence to as many individual, less abstract words as you can.
3. Again share your list with others who have completed this exercise. See whether you understand each other's less abstract statements more clearly than the original ones, and see whether your more concrete statements generate less disagreement.

1. Women are _____

2. Men are _____

3. Government is _____

4. Drugs are _____

5. College is _____

6. Work is _____

1. Women

   a. _____   f. _____

   b. _____   g. _____

   c. _____   h. _____

   d. _____   i. _____

   e. _____   j. _____

2. Men

   a. _____   f. _____

   b. _____   g. _____

   c. _____   h. _____

   d. _____   i. _____

   e. _____   j. _____

3. Government

   a. _____   f. _____

   b. _____   g. _____

   c. _____   h. _____

   d. _____   i. _____

   e. _____   j. _____

4. Drugs

   a. _____   f. _____

   b. _____   g. _____

   c. _____   h. _____

   d. _____   i. _____

   e. _____   j. _____

5. College

a. _____ f. _____

b. _____ g. _____

c. _____ h. _____

d. _____ i. _____

e. _____ j. _____

6. Work

a. _____ f. _____

b. _____ g. _____

c. _____ h. _____

d. _____ i. _____

e. _____ j. _____

▲ 5.4 CONJUGATING IRREGULAR VERBS

PURPOSE

To help you identify the emotive, connotation-laden nature of many apparently impartial, denotative words.

INSTRUCTIONS

1. Demonstrate how the connotative meaning of the terms below can be changed by picking alternate words.
2. Find examples of connotative labeling from your experience.

EXAMPLES

I'm _casual._ _____
You're _a little careless._ _____
He's _a slob._ _____

I'm _thrifty._ _____
You're _money conscious._ _____
She's _a tightwad._ _____

1. I'm tactful.

   You're _____

   He's _____

2. I'm _____

   You're _____

   She's stubborn.

3. I'm _____

   You're a little tipsy.

   He's _____

4. My child is high-spirited.

   Your child is _____

   Their child is _____

5. I'm _____

   You're _____

   He's on an ego trip.

6. I _____

   You slipped up a little on that.

   He _____

7. I'm relaxed.

   You're _____

   She's _____

8. I read _____

   You read erotic literature.

   She reads _____

9. I'm open-minded.

   You're _____

   He's _____

10. I'm cautious.

    You're _____

    She's _____

APPLICATION

Record three examples from your experience in which a speaker used emotive language, labeling his/her/your attitude toward a person, object, or event while giving the appearance of objectively describing it.

1. _____

   _____

   _____

   _____

2. _____

   _____

   _____

   _____

3. _____

   _____

   _____

   _____

▲ 5.5 BEHAVIORAL DESCRIPTIONS

PURPOSE

To increase the clarity of your language by using behavioral descriptions.

INSTRUCTIONS

In each of the situations below, describe the behavior of an individual that might have led to the statement about him or her.

EXAMPLES

John's full of action.
John rode his bike for an hour and then mowed the lawn.
Meg is so much fun to be with.
Meg went shopping in the mall with me and laughed with me about how we looked in the new, looser styles.

1. That teacher is a bore!

   _____

   _____

2. That guy's real macho.

   _____

   _____

3. She's an all-around good person.

   _____

   _____

4. Mike's a hard worker.

   _____

   _____

5. Mark's real laid back.

   _____

   _____

6. Jill's such a dresser.

_____

_____

7. Josh is a real sport.

_____

_____

8. She gives me moral support.

_____

_____

9. Jack's motivated.

_____

_____

10. Peg is inspiring.

_____

_____

11. My parents are understanding.

_____

_____

12. Shelley's a flake!

_____

_____

13. You're too emotional.

_____

_____

14. He's so thoughtful.

_____

_____

▲ 5.6 OPERATIONAL DEFINITIONS

PURPOSE

To increase the clarity of your language by using operational definitions to describe an idea or act.

INSTRUCTIONS

For each of the statements below, write an operational definition of the idea or act to clarify to your partner your intentions.

EXAMPLE

"Go over that way."
"Go across the footbridge, turn right, and go to the third building on your left."

1. Clean up your act.

   _____

   _____

2. This time, clean the car correctly.

   _____

   _____

3. Look more confident.

   _____

   _____

4. You add a bit of this and that and the sauce is finished.

   _____

   _____

5. This paper should be creative.

   _____

   _____

6. Make that report clearer.

_____

_____

7. Work harder on your studies.

_____

_____

8. Pay more attention.

_____

_____

9. Don't be so obnoxious!

_____

_____

10. Don't say things like that.

_____

_____

11. Clean up your room.

_____

_____

12. Be kind to your sister.

_____

_____

13. Get something good at the video store.

_____

_____

14. Fix a healthy dinner.

_____

_____

15. Show me that you care.

_____

_____

▲ 5.7 USING LOWER-LEVEL ABSTRACTIONS

PURPOSES

1. To help you identify ways your language reflects degrees of liking and responsibility.
2. To help you identify high-level abstractions you may use in your everyday language.
3. To help you reduce the high-level abstractions to lower-level abstractions.

INSTRUCTIONS

1. Consider communication-related situations from your life involving people important to you. Pick one situation or a recurring situation that you notice in detail (particular patterns of interaction at breakfast, for example).
2. Write a paragraph about the situation, using high-level abstractions that have *positive* connotations. Underline the abstractions as you write.
3. Write a second paragraph about the *same* situation, this time using high-level abstractions with *negative* connotations. Underline the abstractions as you write them.
4. Write a third paragraph about the *same* situation. This time try to lower the level of abstraction for all the words you found you underlined in paragraphs one and two.
5. Summarize what you learned about your use of abstract language at the end of this exercise. Comment on what degree of liking and responsibility your everyday language reflects.

EXAMPLE

High-level, positive abstractions *My* best friend *from my home town is a* real sweetheart. *In the first place, she's so thoughtful—always calling to see how I'm doing or sending* notes of affection. *She's also* interested in my progress and relays this information to friends back home. *She* maintains our friendship *by* periodic surprise visits *to me here at college.*

High-level, negative abstractions *My ex-friend from home can be a* real pain. *She's always* bugging me—interrupting *me with* late-night calls *and sending me* dumb, childish cards. *She* butts into my business, *too—and has the gall to tell people who don't have any business knowing about my lifestyle and grades.*
She's really inconsiderate, *too—barging in without notice* on me for *free-loader weekends* frequently.

Low-level abstractions *Sue from Sacramento is a person I've known since high school. She still calls me once a week on Thursdays about 9 p.m.; she also sends me one or two Hallmark cards every week. Last week I found out she told my old boyfriend Phil that I was dating four different men and had a 2.0 GPA. Once a month, Sue comes to spend Saturday and Sunday at my apartment.*

Summary *After writing these paragraphs, I realize that I often use the types of abstractions found in the first two paragraphs. In fact, when I'm really glad to see Sue or hear from her, I sound like the writer of the first paragraph, but when I'm feeling hassled or like being left alone, I sound like the writer of the second. I'm sure I must use some high-level abstractions with Sue, too, which must be confusing to her when she tries to figure out how much I like or don't like her. It's easy to see how my degree of liking is reflected in the positive vs. negative paragraphs, but I also think it also shows that I put the responsibility for the interaction with Sue on her when I'm upset, either with her or myself. Writing the low-level abstractions paragraph really helped me define for myself what Sue does, and I think this will enable me to tell her more clearly what I like and don't like.*

High-level, positive abstractions _____

_____

_____

_____

_____

_____

High-level, negative abstractions _____

_____

_____

_____

_____

_____

Low-level abstractions _____

_____

_____

_____

_____

_____

Summary _____

_____

_____

_____

_____

_____

▲ 5.8 DEFINING PROBLEMS AND GOALS BEHAVIORALLY

PURPOSES

1. To give you practice in constructing behavioral descriptions.
2. To help you identify a personal communication problem and construct a goal to correct that problem.
3. To demonstrate that constructing behavioral goals can often help you achieve those goals.

INSTRUCTIONS

Follow the step-by-step directions below.
1. Begin by choosing an aspect of your interpersonal communication with which you are dissatisfied. Record your choice.

EXAMPLE

I don't say "no" when I should. _____

Your problem _____

_____

_____

2. For the next several days, record specific instances in which your problem occurs. Use the form below to be sure that you are noting all important information. Keep recording until you have at least five examples of the problem.

Who Is Involved?	In What Circumstances Does the Problem Occur?	How Did You Behave?
Examples		
My friend N.	Asked to borrow my car.	Said it was low on gas. When she said she'd put some in I sighed and said OK, even though I didn't want to.
My roommate	Asked me if I'd mind doing the dishes when it was her turn so she wouldn't be late for a date. (She does this often.)	Said in quiet, tentative way that this must be the tenth time she's asked. When she said it was really important, I said OK.

Who Is Involved?	In What Circumstances Does the Problem Occur?	How Did You Behave?

3. Summarize the examples you have recorded and rewrite your problem in concrete, behavioral terms.

EXAMPLE

With whom does it occur? *With friends and family, especially my roommate, N., and G.*
In what circumstances does it occur? *When I'm asked to do a favor which I'd rather not do.*
How do you behave? *I usually make a single feeble protest (often by hinting), and then give in if the other person persists.*

With whom does it occur? _____

_____

In what circumstances does it occur? _____

_____

_____

How do you behave? _____

_____

_____

4. Based on the problem statement you have just written, develop a behavioral goal which describes how you would like to act in the target situation you have selected.

EXAMPLE

When friends or family (especially roommate, N., and G.) ask me to do them a favor and I'm not willing, I want to say that I'd rather not do what they ask and explain why. If they persist in asking, I'll continue to say no in a polite but firm way, repeating my explanation if necessary.
I'll remind myself (self-talk) that I have a right to decline requests.

Your behavioral goal

_____

_____

_____

_____

_____

5. For the next several days, record a number of incidents in which you have a chance to practice your target behavior. Try to behave as you have described above, but don't expect to behave perfectly. Remember, you are changing a habit, and old habits die hard. Try to increase the percentage of times you behave in your target manner.

Who Is Involved?	Circumstances	Your Behavior	Comments
Example My friend N.	Invited me to have "a few beers" the day before my Speech midterm.	I repeatedly told him that I needed to study. Persisted despite his insistence.	I'm proud of myself for not giving in. Next time I should try to decline in a more pleasant tone of voice, though.

▲ 5.9   ORAL SKILL CHECK— SPEAKING IN LOW-LEVEL ABSTRACTIONS

PURPOSES

1. To identify high-level abstractions you may use in your everyday life.
2. To give you practice in reducing those high-level abstractions to low-level ones.
3. To demonstrate the value of using low-level abstractions.

INSTRUCTIONS

1. Identify a situation from your personal experience that involves (or has involved) the use of high-level abstraction statements. It may be a situation involving levels of liking and responsibility, one that has to do with defining problems and goals, or one involving power or gender differences in language. Prepare the following for class presentation or to be videotaped.
2. Send your messages in high-level abstractions to a partner. Evaluate the probable outcome of this in real life.
3. Next, send your message to your partner in low-level abstractions. Evaluate the probable outcome.
4. Identify for the class (or the videotape) the high- and low-level abstractions you used. Summarize the advantages of using lower-level abstractions in the situation you selected. If you found few advantages, make a case for using high-level abstractions in this particular instance.

▲ 5.10 CHECKLIST FOR ORAL SKILL—SPEAKING IN LOW-LEVEL ABSTRACTIONS

PURPOSES

1. To identify high-level abstractions you may use in your everyday life.
2. To give you practice in reducing those high-level abstractions to low-level ones.
3. To demonstrate the value of using low-level abstractions.

INSTRUCTIONS

1. Using the instructions in *5.9 Oral skill —Speaking in Low-Level Abstractions,* prepare a situation involving messages of high- and low-level abstractions.
2. Deliver your examples of high- and low-level abstractions to the class.
3. Identify the high- and low-level abstractions you use, evaluating the probable outcome of using each type.
4. Describe the advantages and disadvantages of your low-level abstraction messages.

CHECKLIST

5 = superior   4 = excellent   3 = good   2 = fair   1 = poor

Engages in appropriate nonverbal behavior

    —speaks loud enough to be heard _____

    —looks at audience _____

    —facial expressions consistent with message _____

Sends a message using high-level abstractions _____

Identifies the high-level abstractions, evaluating the probable outcome _____

Sends the same message using low-level abstraction statements _____

Identifies the low-level abstractions, evaluating the probable outcome _____

Describes the advantages/disadvantages of the low-level abstractions _____

                Total _____

▲ 5.11 PRACTICING "I" LANGUAGE

PURPOSE

To give you practice speaking descriptively, instead of evaluatively.

INSTRUCTIONS

Rewrite each of the evaluative "you" language statements below using descriptive "I" language.

EXAMPLE 1

"You don't care about my feelings."
"I felt hurt when I saw you in the restaurant with your old girlfriend. I'm worried that you might want to get back together with her."

EXAMPLE 2

"That was a dumb move!"
"Ever since you used the high setting to dry my favorite cotton shirt, it doesn't fit me anymore. That's why I'm so mad."

1. "Don't ever do that again."

_____

_____

_____

2. "You're awfully sloppy."

_____

_____

_____

3. "Why can't you be more reasonable?"

_____

_____

_____

4. "All you do is talk about yourself."

_____

_____

_____

5. "I wish you'd try to be on time."

_____

_____

_____

6. "You're always taking but never giving."

_____

_____

_____

7. "You have no respect for my belongings!"

_____

_____

_____

8. "You don't listen to me."

_____

_____

_____

9. "Don't be so sensitive."

_____

_____

_____

10. "If you were a real friend, you wouldn't gossip about me."

_____

_____

_____

11. "Why don't you keep your promises?"

_____

_____

_____

12. "Why won't you be honest with me?"

_____

_____

_____

13. "You're unreliable."

_____

_____

_____

14. "You need to develop a little humility."

_____

_____

_____

15. "Why don't you just kick me while I'm down?"

_____

_____

NAME _____

▲ 5.12 CHECKLIST FOR ORAL SKILL—USING "I" LANGUAGE

PURPOSE

To give you practice speaking descriptively, using "I" language.

INSTRUCTIONS

1. Using situations developed in *5.11 Practicing "I" Language* or situations of your own, prepare to deliver both "you" and "I" statements to a partner.
2. Deliver a "you" message to a partner, evaluating its probable outcome
3. Deliver the same message in "I" language to your partner, evaluating its probable outcome.

CHECKLIST

5 = superior   4 = excellent   3 = good   2 = fair   1 = poor

Faces partner and maintains appropriate eye contact   _____

Uses appropriate tone of voice and other nonverbal behaviors   _____

Delivers a "you" message to a partner, evaluating its probable outcome   _____

Delivers the same message in "I" language   _____
   —describes other's specific behavior(s)
   —describes own reactions to other's behavior(s)
   —clearly uses language that accepts responsibility for reaction

Evaluates probable outcome of "I" language   _____

                                                          Total   _____

▲ 5.13 IDENTIFYING LANGUAGE TYPES

PURPOSE

To give you practice in identifying types of language.

INSTRUCTIONS

1. Match the letter of the language type with its description found below.
2. Check your answers in the back of this manual on page 282.

Label the examples of language given below by writing the letter of the language type illustrated on the line in front of the example.

a. inference
b. relative word
c. euphemism
d. emotive word
e. equivocal language

_____ 1. John didn't call **so he must be angry**.

_____ 2. I have a **stomach problem**.

_____ 3. That place is **expensive**.

_____ 4. That guy is a real **hunk**.

_____ 5. I'd like **recognition** for my work.

_____ 6. The bathroom **needs some air**.

_____ 7. We need to make **progress** tonight.

_____ 8. The funeral director pointed out the **slumber room**.

_____ 9. He showed up, **so he must agree**.

_____ 10. That's a real **smart trick you pulled**.

_____ 11. My brother is a **sanitation engineer**.

_____ 12. Ian gave a **long** speech.

_____ 13. My grandfather is **young**.

_____ 14. My sister is a **pill**.

▲ 5.14 IDENTIFYING ABSTRACT LANGUAGE

PURPOSE

To give you practice in identifying abstract language.

INSTRUCTIONS

1. Choose the letter of the *least* abstract alternative to the high abstraction terms.
2. Check your answers in the back of this manual on page 282.

_____   1. Jo's **constantly complaining**.
   a. Jo whines a lot.
   b. Jo complains often about the workload.
   c. Jo told the me three times this week that she feels overworked.
   d. Every time we meet Jo complains about all the work she does.

_____   2. He can **never** do **anything** because he's **always busy**.
   a. He couldn't take me to the dinner because he had to work.
   b. He can never do anything fun because he's always working.
   c. He didn't ever take time off to be with me.
   d. He works too much so we have a boring life.

_____   3. There are **a lot of problems** associated with **freedom**.
   a. Freedom carries with it responsibility.
   b. Since I moved into my own apartment, I have to pay ten bills.
   c. I don't like all the responsibility of living on my own.
   d. My economic responsibilities limit my freedom.

_____   4. Shannon is **worthless** as a roommate.
   a. Shannon is always gone, so she's really not part of our house.
   b. Shannon never does her part around here.
   c. Shannon's jobs seldom get done around here.
   d. Shannon has attended only one of our six house meetings.

_____   5. Carlos is the **most wonderful friend**.
   a. Carlos has never told anyone about my fear of failing.
   b. Carlos listens to me about everything.
   c. Carlos is the best listener I've ever met.
   d. I can trust Carlos implicitly with all my secrets.

C H A P T E R   S I X

▲ **Nonverbal Communication:** ▲
Messages without Words

▲ I. NONVERBAL COMMUNICATION
   A. **Social Importance**
      1. Mehrabian: 93 percent
      2. Birdwhistle: 65 percent
   B. **Definition: Those Messages Expressed by Other Than Linguistic Means**

II. CHARACTERISTICS OF NONVERBAL COMMUNICATION
   A. **Nonverbal Communication Exists**
      1. Deliberate
      2. Unintentional
   C. **Nonverbal Communication Is Culture-Bound**
   D. **Nonverbal Communication Is Primarily Relational**
   E. **Nonverbal Communication Serves Many Functions**
      1. Repeating
      2. Substituting
      3. Complementing
      4. Accenting
      5. Regulating
      6. Contradicting
   F. **Nonverbal Communication Is Ambiguous**

III. DIFFERENCES BETWEEN VERBAL AND NONVERBAL COMMUNICATION
   A. **Single vs. Multiple Channels**
   B. **Discrete vs. Continuous**
   C. **Clear vs. Ambiguous**
   D. **Verbal vs. Nonverbal Impact**
   E. **Deliberate vs. Unconscious**

IV. TYPES OF NONVERBAL COMMUNICATION

A. Body Orientation

B. Posture
1. Forward/backward lean
2. Tension/relaxation

C. Gestures
1. Preening behaviors
2. Manipulators

D. Face and Eyes
1. Complexity
2. Speed
3. Emotions reflected
4. Microexpression
5. Kinds of messages
   a. Involvement
   b. Positive/negative attitude
   c. Dominance/submission
   d. Interest (pupils)

E. Voice (Paralanguage): Tone, Speed, Pitch, Number and Length of Pauses, Volume, Disfluencies

F. Touch

G. Clothing

H. Proxemics (Space)
1. Intimate
2. Personal
3. Social
4. Public

I. Territoriality

J. Physical Environment

K. Time (Chronemics)

▲ KEY TERMS

accenting
ambiguous messages
chronemics
complementing
contradicting
deception cues
disfluencies
double messages
emblems
gestures

illustrators
intimate distance
kinesics
leakage
manipulators
microexpressions
nonverbal communication
paralanguage
personal distance
posture

preening behavior
proxemics
public distance
regulating
relaxation cue

repeating
social distance
substituting
tension cue
territory

▲ 6.1 DESCRIBING NONVERBAL STATES

PURPOSE

To describe the nonverbal behaviors that indicate emotional and attitudinal states.

INSTRUCTIONS

1. For each of the statements below, record the verbal behavior that goes along with it (if none, record silence).
2. Then make a list of the nonverbal behaviors that indicate to you that a person is feeling or acting that way.
3. Compare your responses with those of others in the class and note the similarities and differences in your responses.

Statement	Verbal Behavior	Nonverbal Behavior
Example She listens well.	"Uh, huh." "Yeah"	Turns body toward me, leans forward, smiles once or twice, nods, maintains eye contact about 80 percent of the time.
1. He acts so cool.		
2. She's a tease.		
3. He's paranoid.		
4. She's flirting.		

Statement	Verbal Behavior	Nonverbal Behavior
5. He's stressing out.		
6. She takes over.		
7. He's overdramatic.		
8. She acts confident.		
9. He seems friendly.		
10. She's "hyper."		

COMPARISONS

Record the similarities and differences you found in comparing your responses to those of your classmates. Which nonverbal behaviors did you notice that others did not and vice versa?

_____

_____

_____

_____

▲ 6.2 NONVERBAL COMPLAINTS

PURPOSE

To facilitate the display of nonverbally congruent behaviors.

INSTRUCTIONS

For each of the common complaints below, list nonverbal communication advice that *may* work for the person complaining. Compare your advice with that of others in the class, noting the differences different people or contexts may have on the advice.

Complaint	Nonverbal Advice
Example He says I'm too eager to please.	Take a little more time to respond after a request. Lean toward the person a little less. Smile, but don't keep the smile on your face continuously. Gesture, but don't gesture as quickly. Stand a little more erect and hold all the parts of your body more still.
1. She says I'm too serious.	
2. My boss says not to be so aggressive.	
3. He says I could act more helpful.	
4. Friend or relative says I don't really care about him/her.	
5. I sound stupid when I hear myself on tape.	

Complaint	Nonverbal Advice
6. They look so sure of themselves, but I just can't act that way.	
7. I'd like to look more relaxed.	
8. I don't want them to think I'm indifferent.	
9. She says I act too cold.	
10. He says I should be more open.	

Compare your advice with that of others in the class. Note any similarities or differences.

_____

_____

_____

_____

How might the persons involved or the context change the advice you would give?

_____

_____

_____

_____

▲ 6.3 NONVERBAL HOW-TO'S

PURPOSE

To define what you and others in the class consider effective nonverbal behavior in some social situations.

INSTRUCTIONS

1. For each of the social situations below, list the nonverbal behaviors you believe will effectively communicate what is desired.
2. Compare your answers with those of others in your class.
3. Reflect on the behavior of yourself and others important to you; how might you change some of the nonverbal cues you display to communicate what you desire more effectively?

Social Situations	Nonverbal Behaviors
Example Initiate conversation with a stranger at a party.	Make eye contact, offer hand in greeting, smile, come within four feet of other person, turn body toward other person, nod occasionally when other is talking.
1. Take control or exercise leadership in a class group.	
2. Come across well in a job interview.	
3. Tell an interesting joke or story.	
4. Appear friendly and warm.	

Social Situation	Nonverbal Behaviors
5. Signal your desire to leave a conversation when the other person keeps on talking.	
6. Appear confident when asking boss for a raise.	
7. Appear interested in class lecture.	
8. Avoid talking with an undesirable person.	
9. Let a friend know you need to leave.	
10. Appear concerned about a friend's dilemma.	

Compare your answers with others in class. Note the areas of agreement and disagreement.

_____

_____

_____

_____

_____

_____

Are there situations or contexts in which the described behaviors would be changed to appear "effective?"

_____

_____

_____

_____

_____

How might you or someone close to you change nonverbal behaviors to more effectively communicate the desired idea?

_____

_____

_____

_____

_____

_____

_____

▲ 6.4 OBSERVING NONVERBAL BEHAVIOR

PURPOSE

To help you observe and record nonverbal behaviors and classify the nonverbal behaviors according to type.

INSTRUCTIONS

1. Observe people engaging in the behaviors indicated below. (You may search out these situations yourself, or your instructor may have two people from the class role-play each of these situations for you to observe in class.)
2. Describe the verbal behavior briefly in the first column. Give a specific quote or summarize the content of the conversation.
3. Describe the nonverbal behaviors that went along with the verbal behavior. Be sure to be specific about the behaviors and avoid interpretations. ("She looked angry.")
4. Classify each of the nonverbal behaviors according to the following types:
   body orientation
   posture
   gestures
   face and eyes
   voice
   touch
   clothing
   proxemics
   territoriality
   physical environment

SITUATION 1: COMPLAINING

Two students are talking with one another about some of their instructors. One student begins to complain to the other about a particular instructor.

Verbal Behavior	Nonverbal Behaviors	Type
Example		
Jim is saying how bad Prof. X is.	Jim leaned forward.	Posture
	His tone of voice went up.	Voice
	He shook his head.	Kinesics
	His eyes squinted.	Eyes
	He put his hand up and moved it forward to emphasize words.	Gestures

SITUATIONS 2: GREETING BEHAVIORS

Two friends see one another, greet, and begin to talk about what they have done since the last time they saw one another.

Verbal Behavior	Nonverbal Behaviors	Type

SITUATION 3: LEAVE-TAKING BEHAVIORS

Two students are seated, talking about a class, when one of them remembers that s/he is late for an appointment.

Verbal Behavior	Nonverbal Behaviors	Type

SITUATION 4: EXPLAINING

One student approaches another, asking for directions to the administration building. The second student gives the directions.

Verbal Behavior	Nonverbal Behaviors	Type

SITUATION 5: LISTENING

Two friends are sitting in class before it begins. One is telling about the date s/he had last night; the other is listening intently. Record the listening behavior.

Verbal Behavior	Nonverbal Behaviors	Type

▲ 6.5 NONVERBAL COMMUNICATION IN THE MEDIA

PURPOSES

1. To give you practice describing nonverbal behaviors.
2. To illustrate the diversity of nonverbal behavior.
3. To help you discover the messages you get from the nonverbal behavior of people on television.

INSTRUCTIONS

Observe three different types of television programs (news show, game show, drama, soap opera, children's show, documentary, situation comedy, or mystery, for example). Watch just a segment of each and describe the nonverbal behaviors of one or two main people; then compare the nonverbal behaviors to see if you can get clusters of nonverbal cues that get across a certain attitude or concept or feeling.

MEDIA 1

Name of show _____

Nonverbal behaviors observed

_____

_____

_____

_____

_____

MEDIA 2

Name of show _____

Nonverbal behaviors observed

_____

_____

_____

_____

_____

MEDIA 3

Name of show _____

Nonverbal behaviors observed

_____

_____

_____

_____

_____

Compare the sets of behaviors you have described above. What are the similarities and differences?

_____

_____

_____

_____

_____

_____

Can you find clusters of nonverbal cues that communicate seriousness versus lightheartedness or other types of feelings, attitudes, or concepts?

_____

_____

_____

_____

_____

_____

▲ 6.6 CHECKING YOUR NONVERBAL INTERPRETATIONS

PURPOSES

1. To demonstrate the ambiguity of nonverbal messages.
2. To increase your understanding of others' nonverbal behavior.

INSTRUCTIONS

1. For the next several days, pay special attention to the nonverbal behavior of a significant other. (If you are not able to observe a single significant person, you may spread your observations among several others.)
2. Note your interpretation of your subject's nonverbal behaviors. At an appropriate time, share your interpretation with the other person, and see if it is accurate.
3. At the end of your observation period, summarize your findings in the space provided below.

CONCLUSIONS

In what circumstances are your interpretations of others' nonverbal behaviors accurate? (Specify certain people, behaviors, and situations.)

_____

_____

_____

_____

_____

In what circumstances are your interpretations likely to be inaccurate? (Specify certain people, behaviors, and situations.)

_____

_____

_____

_____

_____

Situation	Other's Nonverbal Behavior	Your Interpretation of the Behavior	Result of Checking Your Interpretation/Perception
Example Several of us were celebrating the arrival of Friday at my place by having a few beers.	My friend S. was much more quiet than usual and snapped at me in a harsh voice and scowled when I tried to kid him about his low consumption of beer.	I figured he must be mad at me for not loaning him my car earlier that week.	After everyone else had gone, I told S. what I suspected. He said that he was angry, but at himself and not me. He hadn't studied for a test and had blown it. He apologized for spreading his gloom.
1.			
2.			
3.			
4.			
5.			

NAME _____

▲ 6.7 NONVERBAL FUNCTIONS

PURPOSES

1. To help you recognize the functions of nonverbal behaviors in your own life.
2. To identify each of the six functions of nonverbal behavior you and others around you use.

INSTRUCTIONS

1. Observe an example of each of the six functions of nonverbal communication listed below.
2. For each function, describe the persons involved, the setting, and the verbal and nonverbal behaviors exhibited by the people involved.
3. Describe the effects of the congruency or incongruency of verbal and nonverbal messages in the conclusions section below.

CONCLUSIONS

What are the results for you and others where verbal and nonverbal behavior are congruent (repeats, complements) vs. where they are incongruent (contradicts)?

_____

_____

_____

_____

_____

Function	Persons Involved	Setting	Verbal Behavior	Nonverbal Behavior
Repeats				
Substitutes for				
Complements				
Accents				
Regulates				
Contradicts				

▲ 6.8 NONVERBAL INTERVIEW

PURPOSE

To help you become aware of the ways you express emotions nonverbally to a significant other.

INSTRUCTIONS

1. Choose one significant other as your interview partner. This should be someone with whom you interact on a frequent basis.
2. Ask your partner to tell you how s/he observes or "knows" when you are feeling three different emotions (have him/her pick three emotions from the list below, or decide with your partner on the three you will discuss).
3. Using the forms below, record the nonverbal channels your partner notices for each emotion.
4. After completing the observation phase, summarize your findings in the space provided.

EMOTIONAL STATE 1 _____

Facial expressions	
Gestures	
Postures	
Body orientation	
Distance	
Voice	
Clothing	
Touch	

EMOTIONAL STATE 2 _____

Facial expressions	
Gestures	
Postures	
Body orientation	
Distance	
Voice	
Clothing	
Touch	

EMOTIONAL STATE 3 _____

Facial expressions	
Gestures	
Postures	
Body orientation	
Distance	
Voice	
Clothing	
Touch	

CONCLUSIONS

Based on your discussion with your partner and your observations here, which emotions do you exhibit most often?

_____

_____

Which channels do you use to express each of the above-mentioned emotional states?

_____

_____

_____

_____

_____

In what situations do your expressions of emotional states usually occur?

_____

_____

_____

_____

_____

How accurately did your partner "judge" your emotions? Are there reasons why you think s/he was a good or poor "nonverbal reader?"

_____

_____

_____

_____

_____

▲ 6.9 CONGRUENT MESSAGES

PURPOSE

To match verbal and nonverbal behaviors to send congruent messages.

INSTRUCTIONS

1. In each of the following situations, describe your likely verbal and nonverbal behaviors necessary to make the interpersonal situation *congruent*. Use descriptions of the ten types of nonverbal communication described in Chapter 6 of *Looking Out/Looking In* (e.g., posture, gesture, etc.).
2. Describe four situations from your own life and how you would send the optimum blend of congruent and/or incongruent verbal and nonverbal messages.

Situation	Your Verbal Behavior	Your Nonverbal Behavior	How Congruent Are the Verbal/Nonverbal Messages?	Possible Consequences of this Congruency/Incongruency
Example Person I like a lot takes me out to dinner and I have a good time and enjoy the food.	"I'm really enjoying this; the food is terrific and so is the company."	I look at my partner when I talk, smiling and tilting my head slightly forward. I lean toward my partner and touch my partner lightly on the arm and hand.	My verbal and nonverbal behaviors are very congruent in this context.	I hope the consequences are that my partner will understand how much I care and enjoy our time together. I run the risk of not "game playing" of course—in that I could be hurt if my partner's feelings don't match mine, but I think the chances are pretty slim in this instance.
1. My boss calls me into the office to tell me what a good job I've been doing lately.				
2. My roommate has dinner ready when I get home after a rough day.				
3. My father drops in to visit me when my lover is over for the evening.				
4. My lab partner suggests that we go out partying together Friday night.				
5. My sister or brother asks to borrow my favorite sweater for a big date.				

CHAPTER SIX ▲ Nonverbal Communication: Messages without Words **167**

Situation of Your Own	Your Optimal Verbal Behavior	Your Optimal Nonverbal Behavior	Congruency/Incongruency
1.			
2.			
3.			
4.			

In what situations is it wise, and when is it unwise, to express your emotions "congruently"?

_____

_____

_____

_____

_____

In what situations is congruity desirable? How could you best match your verbal and nonverbal behaviors in these situations?

_____

_____

_____

_____

_____

Based on your observations in this exercise, when are you least aware of the emotions (describe which ones) you express only nonverbally?

_____

_____

_____

_____

_____

▲ 6.10 ORAL SKILL—
OBSERVING CONGRUENT/INCONGRUENT BEHAVIOR

1. Recognize the large amount of behavior that is observable whenever two or more people communicate.
2. Become more accurate at reporting behavior to others.
3. Understand how behavior forms the basis for your interpretations of others' behavior.
4. Judge the congruent/incongruent behaviors of others.

INSTRUCTIONS

1. Form groups of four members. Designate the first person A, the next B, and the other two as observers.
2. For a period of five minutes the observers record all the behavior they observe about A and B as they discuss one of the topics on the following page. For example, "Now I see Nick smiling . . . Now I notice Alice shifting in her seat . . . Now I hear Cheryl sigh . . . Now I'm aware of Bob looking at the clock."
3. After observing, the observers rank A and B as to the congruency of the reported behavior they observed.
4. Now A and B become the observers, and the others become A and B. Again, the observers record the verbal and nonverbal behaviors. For example, "Now I see Bob grimace and I think he's feeling nervous about being next to do this assignment . . . Now I hear Cheryl laugh, and I think she agrees with my guess about Bob."
5. Complete the rankings on all group members.
6. Discuss the desirability of congruent and incongruent behavior in each of the studied situations.

▲ 6.11 CHECKLIST FOR ORAL SKILL— CONGRUENT/INCONGRUENT BEHAVIOR

INSTRUCTIONS

1. In dyads, discuss one of the following topics for five minutes while the other dyad observes you:
   music
   films
   literature
   drugs
   sex

2. Observers will record nonverbal behaviors and verbal behaviors on a separate sheet of paper and then rank each dyadic partner as to the *congruency* of his/her verbal and nonverbal behaviors during discussion. Use the following ranking scale:

Highly congruent   5   4   3   2   1   Highly incongruent

Rate the *congruency* of verbal behavior with each of the nonverbal categories listed below.	Person A	Person B
1. Facial expression	_____	_____
2. Eye contact	_____	_____
3. Posture	_____	_____
4. Paralanguage	_____	_____
5. Body orientation	_____	_____
6. Distance	_____	_____
7. Touch	_____	_____
8. Gestures	_____	_____

3. Switch roles as observers/participants; rank the new participants as to their congruency after recording their verbal and nonverbal behaviors.

4. As a foursome, discuss the desirability/undesirability of congruent versus incongruent verbal and nonverbal behavior in each of the situations observed (i.e., are high rankings of congruency necessarily desirable in each situation?).

▲ 6.12 IDENTIFYING TYPES OF NONVERBAL COMMUNICATION

PURPOSE

To give you practice in identifying types of nonverbal communication.

INSTRUCTIONS

1. Match the letter of the type of nonverbal communication with an example of the type found below.
2. Check your answers in the back of this manual on page 282.

    a. kinesics   c. proxemics   e. environment
    b. paralinguistics   d. territoriality

_____   1.   The executive stared at her employee.

_____   2.   Jeremy put a "NO ENTRANCE" sign on his door.

_____   3.   The students rearranged the chairs in the classroom.

_____   4.   Anne stepped back three feet from her friend.

_____   5.   Martin turned his body away from his brother.

_____   6.   Rob's voice softened when he spoke to her.

_____   7.   There was a long pause after the decision was made.

_____   8.   Mitchell sighed audibly.

_____   9.   Gretchen took the seat three down from Rachel.

_____   10.   Kevin was annoyed that someone was leaning on his car.

_____   11.   The roommates decorated with posters and lights.

_____   12.   The officer pointed in the correct direction.

_____   13.   The lovers were sitting only inches apart.

_____   14.   No one dared to sit in Ralph's chair.

▲ LISTENING: MORE THAN MEETS THE EAR ▲

▲ I. **LISTENING IS IMPORTANT**

II. **ELEMENTS IN THE LISTENING PROCESS**
   A. Hearing
   B. Attending
   C. Understanding
   D. Responding
   E. Remembering

III. **TYPES OF NONLISTENING**
   A. Pseudolistening
   B. Stage Hogging
   C. Selective Listening
   D. Insulated Listening
   E. Defensive Listening
   F. Ambushing
   G. Insensitive Listening

IV. **WHY WE DON'T LISTEN**
   A. Message Overload
   B. Preoccupation
   C. Rapid Thought
   D. Effort
   E. External Noise
   F. Hearing Problems

G. **Faulty Assumptions**
   1. Heard it all before
   2. Speaker's words too simple
   3. Speaker's words too complex
   4. Subject is uninteresting

H. **Lack of Apparent Advantages**
   1. Control
   2. Admiration/respect
   3. Energy release

I. **Lack of Training**

V. **INFORMATIONAL LISTENING**

   A. **Talk Less**

   B. **Get Rid of Distractions**

   C. **Don't Judge Prematurely**

   D. **Look for Key Ideas**

   E. **Ask Questions**

   F. **Paraphrase**

VI. **LISTENING TO HELP**

   A. **Advising**
      1. Be correct
      2. Make sure other is ready to accept
      3. Best is blame is not likely

   B. **Judging**
      1. Asked for judgment
      2. Constructive judgment

   C. **Analyzing**
      1. Be tentative
      2. Have chance of being correct
      3. Receptive other
      4. Motivated to be helpful

   D. **Questioning**
      1. Don't ask out of your own curiosity
      2. Don't confuse or distract
      3. Don't disguise suggestions/criticism

   E. **Supporting**
      1. Be sincere
      2. See if the other can accept the support

   F. **Prompting**

G. Paraphrasing
1. Thoughts
2. Emotions
3. When to use paraphrasing
   a. If the problem is complex enough
   b. If you have necessary time
   c. If you are genuinely interested in helping
   d. If you can withhold judgment
   e. If you're comfortable with style and don't overuse it

H. Which Style to Use?
1. Consider the situation
2. Consider the other person
3. Consider yourself

▲ KEY TERMS

active listening
advising
ambushing
analyzing
attending
conversational narcissist
defensive listening
elements in listening process
hearing
insensitive listening
insulated listening
judging
paraphrasing

parroting
prompting
pseudolistening
questioning response
residual message
responding
selective listening
shift-response
stage hogging
supporting
understanding
verbatim

▲ 7.1 LISTENING DIARY

PURPOSES

1. To help you identify the styles of listening you use in your interpersonal relationships.
2. To help you discover the consequences of the listening styles you use.

BACKGROUND

Looking Out/Looking In identifies several styles of listening and nonlistening which you can use when seeking information from another:

pseudolistening	insensitive listening
stage hogging	ambushing
selective listening	prompting
insulated listening	questioning
defensive listening	paraphrasing

INSTRUCTIONS

1. Use the following form to record the listening styles you use in various situations.
2. After completing your diary, record your conclusions in the space provided.

Time and Place	People	Subject	Listening Style(s)	Consequences
Example Saturday night party	my date and several new acquaintances	good backpacking trips	*stage hogging:* I used everybody's remarks to show what a hotshot explorer I am.	I guess I was trying to get everyone to like me. My egotistical attitude probably accomplished the opposite!
1.				
2.				
3.				

Time and Place	People	Subject	Listening Style(s)	Consequences
4.				
5.				

CONCLUSIONS

Based on your observations here, what styles of listening and nonlistening do you use most often? In what situations do you use each of these styles? (Consider the people involved, the time, subject, and your personal mood when determining situational variables.)

_____

_____

_____

_____

_____

_____

_____

_____

What are the consequences of the listening styles you have just described?

_____

_____

_____

_____

_____

_____

_____

_____

_____

_____

▲ 7.2 RESPONSES TO PROBLEMS

PURPOSE

To help you practice the various styles of responding to others' problems.

INSTRUCTIONS

For each of the problem statements below, write a response in each style of helping discussed in *Looking Out/Looking In*. Make your response as realistic as possible.

EXAMPLE

"I don't know what to do. I tried to explain to my professor why the assignment was late, but he wouldn't even listen to me."

Advising *You ought to write him a note. He might be more open if he has time to read it and think about it.*

Judging *You have to accept these things. Moping won't do any good, so quit feeling sorry for yourself.*

Analyzing *I think the reason he wasn't sympathetic is because he hears lots of excuses this time of year.*

Supporting *All of your work has been so good that I'm sure this one assignment won't matter. Don't worry!*

Questioning *What did he say? Do you think he'll change his mind later? How could you make up the assignment?*

Prompting *(Short silence) And so. . .?*

Paraphrasing *You sound really discouraged, since he didn't even seem to care about your reasons — is that it?*

1. My girlfriend says she wants to date other guys this summer while I'm out in the boondocks working on construction. She claims it's just to keep busy and that it won't make any difference with us, but I think she wants to break off permanently, and she's trying to do it gently.

   Advising _____

   _____

   Judging _____

   _____

   Analyzing _____

   _____

   Supporting _____

   _____

Questioning _____

_____

Prompting _____

_____

Paraphrasing _____

_____

2. My roommate and I can't seem to get along. She's always having her boyfriend over, and he doesn't know when to go home. I don't want to move out, but I can't put up with this much longer. If I bring it up I know my roommate will get defensive, though.

Advising _____

_____

Judging _____

_____

Analyzing _____

_____

Supporting _____

_____

Questioning _____

_____

Prompting _____

_____

Paraphrasing _____

_____

3. What do you do about a friend who borrows things and doesn't return them?

Advising _____

_____

Judging _____

_____

Analyzing _____

_____

Supporting _____

_____

Questioning _____

_____

Prompting _____

_____

Paraphrasing _____

_____

4. The pressure of going to school and doing all the other things in my life is really getting to me. I can't go on like this, but I don't know where I can cut back.

Advising _____

_____

Judging _____

_____

Analyzing _____

_____

Supporting _____

_____

Questioning _____

_____

Prompting _____

_____

Paraphrasing _____

_____

5. You think that by the time you become an adult your parents would stop treating you like a child, but not mine! If I wanted their advice about how to live my life, I'd ask.

Advising _____

_____

Judging _____

_____

Analyzing _____

_____

Supporting _____

_____

Questioning _____

_____

Prompting _____

_____

Paraphrasing _____

_____

▲ 7.3 PARAPHRASING PRACTICE

PURPOSE

To develop your ability to paraphrase in order to gain information about another person's thoughts.

INSTRUCTIONS

Write a paraphrasing response for each of the following statements. Include the speaker's thoughts and, as appropriate, the speaker's feelings.

1. "I guess it's OK for you to use my computer. Just be careful to handle the floppy disks only by the cover, and don't put any food or drinks on the desk or anywhere near the machine. This computer cost me a lot of money, and it would be a disaster if anything happened to it."

   _____

   _____

   _____

2. "You'll have the best chance at getting a loan for the new car you want if you give us a complete financial statement and credit history."

   _____

   _____

   _____

3. (Instructor to student) "This paper shows a lot of promise. It could probably earn you an A grade if you just develop the idea about the problems that arise from poor listening a bit more."

   _____

   _____

   _____

4. "I do like the communication course, but it's not at all what I expected. It's much more *personal*, if you know what I mean."

   _____

   _____

5. "We just got started on your car's transmission. I'm pretty sure we can have it ready tonight."

_____

_____

_____

6. "I do think it's wrong to take any lives, but sometimes I think certain criminals deserve capital punishment."

_____

_____

_____

7. "We are planning to have some friends over tonight, but I guess you're welcome to come too. Why don't you just bring along something we can munch on so we'll be sure to have enough food?"

_____

_____

_____

8. "You know I enjoy spending time with you. But I have other friends, too!"

_____

_____

_____

▲ 7.4 LISTENING FOR FEELINGS

PURPOSE

To help you identify the feelings which are often implied but not stated by others.

INSTRUCTIONS

For each of the statements below, write the feeling or feelings which the speaker might be experiencing.

Possible Feeling(s)	Speaker's Remarks
Example puzzlement, hurt	It seems like you haven't been paying much attention to me lately. Is there something wrong?
1.	1. I wonder if I ought to start looking for another job. They're reorganizing the company, and what with drop in business and all, maybe this is one of the jobs they'll cut back on. But if my boss finds out I'm looking around, maybe he'll think I don't like it here and let me go anyway.
2.	2. It was a great game. I played a lot, I guess, but I only scored once. The coach put Ryan in ahead of me.
3.	3. I said I'd do the collecting for him, but I sure don't feel like it. But I owe him a favor, so I guess I'll have to do it.
4.	4. I've got a report due tomorrow, an exam the next day, rehearsals every night this week, and now a meeting this afternoon. I don't think I can even fit in eating, and this has been going on all month.
5.	5. Sure she gets better grades than I do. She's a housewife, takes only two classes, and all she has to do is study. I have to work a job and go to school, too. And I don't have anyone to support me.
6.	6. I can't understand why they haven't written. They've never been gone this long without at least a card, and I don't even know how to get in touch with them.

Possible Feeling(s)	Speaker's Remarks
7.	7. We had a great evening last night. The dinner was fantastic; so was the party. We saw lots of people; Erin loves that sort of thing.
8.	8. My daughter got straight A's this year, and the high school has a reputation for being very hard. She's a natural student. But sometimes I wonder if she isn't all books. I wish I could help her get interested in something besides studying.
9.	9. Boy, the teacher tells us he'll mark off on our grade every time we're late, but it doesn't seem to bother him when he comes in late. He must figure it's his privilege.
10.	10. I worked up that whole study—did all the surveying, the compiling, the writing. It was my idea in the first place. But he turned it in to the head office with his name on it, and he got the credit.
11.	11. I don't know whether I'm doing a good job or not. She never tells me if I'm doing well or need to work harder. I sure hope she likes my work.
12.	12. She believed everything he said about me. She wouldn't even listen to my side, just started yelling at me.
13.	13. Look, we've gone over and over this. The meeting could have been over an hour ago if we hadn't gotten hung up on this one point. If we can't make a decision, let's table it and move on.
14.	14. Look, I know I acted like a rat. I apologized, and I'm trying to make up for it. I can't do any more, can I? So drop it!
15.	15. How can I tell him how I really feel? He might get mad and then we'd start arguing. He'll think I don't love him if I tell him my real feelings.

▲ 7.5 PROBLEM SOLVING PARAPHRASING

PURPOSE

To help you become skillful at giving paraphrasing responses to others' problems.

BACKGROUND

You have already learned that the most helpful paraphrasing responses reflect both the speaker's thoughts and feelings. In order for this style of helping to be effective, you also have to sound like yourself, and not another person or a robot. There are many ways to reflect another's thoughts and feelings:

"It sounds like you're ..."
"I hear you saying ..."
"Let me see if I've got it. You're saying ..."
"So you're telling me ..."

INSTRUCTIONS

Write a paraphrasing response for each of the statements which follow. Be sure that the response fits your style of speaking, while at the same time it reflects the speaker's *thoughts* and *feelings*.

EXAMPLE

"Stan always wants to tell me about the women he's going out with; he gives me `blow-by-blow' descriptions of their dates that take hours, and he never seems to ask about who I'm going out with or what I'm interested in."
"It seems like you might be tired (feeling) of hearing about Stan's love life (thoughts) and maybe a little put-out (feeling) that he doesn't solicit information from you about whom you're dating (thoughts)—is that it?"

1. "I can't believe it! First the instructor said my answers were too skimpy, so I gave her more information. Now she tells me I'm being too wordy. Arggh!"

   _____

   _____

   _____

2. "What would you do if you heard your best friend making fun of you behind your back?"

   _____

   _____

   _____

3. "We can't decide whether to put grandmother in a nursing home. She hates the idea, but she can't take care of herself anymore, and it's just too much for us."

_____

_____

_____

4. "Those damn finals are finally over. I'm never going to even *think* about history again!"

_____

_____

_____

5. "I'm really starting to hate my job. Every day I do the same boring, mindless work. But if I quit, I might not find any better work."

_____

_____

_____

6. "They haven't called me in ages. I think they must be mad at me or something."

_____

_____

_____

7. "Maybe I'll just use their lawn as a bathroom. Then they'll understand what their dog is doing to my yard!"

_____

_____

_____

8. "Why don't you try to be a little less messy around here? This place looks like a dump!"

_____

_____

_____

▲ 7.6 STYLES OF HELPING DIARY

PURPOSES

1. To help you identify the ways in which you respond to others' problems.
2. To help you identify the consequences of your helping style.

BACKGROUND

Looking Out/Looking In identifies several types of helping responses:

advising	supporting
judging	prompting
analyzing	paraphrasing
questioning	

INSTRUCTIONS

1. Use the following form to record the opportunities you have to help others with their problems and to note the helping style you use and its consequences.
2. After completing your diary, use the space provided to analyze the consequences of your present helping styles, and to decide how you can be more helpful.

Situation	Your Helping Response	Consequences of Your Response
Example My friend M. was expressing anger at the unwillingness of his boss to give him more responsibility on the job.	I offered *advice*. I told M. that I once was in the same situation, and that after trying my best and never being listened to, I finally quit. I told him I was glad I'd done so, and suggested that he might have to do the same thing.	M. didn't seem very enthusiastic about my advice. He didn't object out loud, but his facial expression made me think that he didn't want to quit. I don't think my remarks were very helpful.
1.		
2.		

Situation	Your Helping Response	Consequences of Your Response
3.		
4.		
5.		

CONCLUSIONS

Based on your observations in the preceding diary, what styles of helping do you use most often? In what situations do you use each of these styles? (Consider the people involved, the time, subject, and your personal mood when determining situational variables.)

_____

_____

_____

_____

_____

_____

What are the consequences of the helping styles you have just described? In what cases do they truly help the other person, and when are they not helpful?

_____

_____

_____

_____

_____

_____

How could you change your style of responding in order to be more helpful to others?

_____

_____

_____

_____

_____

_____

▲ 7.7 ORAL SKILL—PARAPHRASING INFORMATION

INSTRUCTIONS

1. Join with three partners to create a foursome. Label the members A, B, C, and D.
2. A and B review the list below, choosing the topic upon which they disagree most widely.
3. A and B conduct a five-minute conversation on the topic they have chosen. During this period, the speakers may not express their own ideas until they have paraphrased the other person's position to his or her satisfaction. (If A and B finish discussing one item, they should move on to a second one from the list below.)
4. During the conversation, C and D should use *7.10 Checklist for Oral Skill—Paraphrasing Information* to observe each of the speakers as follows:
   C observes A   D observes B
5. At the end of the conversation, the observers should review the skill rating with the persons they observed.
6. Steps 1–5 are now repeated with the roles of conversationalists and observers reversed.

TOPICS

Indicate your position on each statement below by circling one of the following labels:

TA = totally agree   A = agree   D = disagree   TD = totally disagree

1. Despite the value of classes like this one, in the last analysis good communicators are born, not made.   TA   A   D   TD

2. One measure of a person's effectiveness as a communicator is how well he or she is liked by others.   TA   A   D   TD

3. No matter how unreasonable or rude they are, people deserve to be treated with respect.   TA   A   D   TD

4. An effective communicator should be able to handle any situation in a way that leaves the other person feeling positive about the interaction.   TA   A   D   TD

5. Interpersonal communication classes should be a required part of everyone's college education.   TA   A   D   TD

6. Most of what is taught in interpersonal communication classes is really common sense.   TA   A   D   TD

OR as an alternative

1. Choose a topic of interest to you and a partner (music, politics, religion, men, women, morals, etc.). It is best if you anticipate some difference of opinion on the topic.
2. Take turns stating your opinion. The only rule is that before you can take your turn stating *your* opinion, you must paraphrase the content of your partner's opinion *to his/her satisfaction.*
3. Use *7.10 Checklist for Oral Skill—Paraphrasing Information* to have yourselves evaluated by your instructor or other students.

▲ 7.8 CHECKLIST FOR ORAL SKILL—PARAPHRASING INFORMATION

PURPOSE

To give you practice paraphrasing for information.

INSTRUCTIONS

Using the conversation in *7.9 Oral Skill—Paraphrasing Information*, discuss the statements with a partner. Your observer should use the checklist below to evaluate your ability to paraphrase information.

CHECKLIST

5 = superior   4 = excellent   3 = good   2 = fair   1 = poor

Uses appropriate nonverbal attending behaviors   _____
    —faces speaker
    —sits upright or leans slightly toward speaker
    —looks at speaker throughout the conversation
    —facial expression indicates interest
    —vocal tone reflects interest

Asks nonleading questions as appropriate   _____

Fluently and concisely paraphrases the speaker's thoughts   _____

Expresses paraphrasing in a tentative manner; invites verification
by the speaker verbally or nonverbally   _____

                                                           Total   _____

▲ 7.9 ORAL SKILL—PARAPHRASING FOR PROBLEM SOLVING

PURPOSE

To give you practice paraphrasing thoughts and feelings.

INSTRUCTIONS

1. With a partner, decide on communication situations that require paraphrasing for problem solving skills (paraphrasing both thoughts and feelings). The situations should be real for the person describing them and might involve a problem you have, a decision you have to make, an issue of importance to you, or a change in a relationship in which you are involved.
2. Have your partner tell you of his/her problem/issue/decision/relationship while you paraphrase thoughts and feelings.
3. You then tell your partner of your problem/issue/decision/relationship while your partner paraphrases your thoughts and feelings.

▲ 7.10 CHECKLIST FOR ORAL SKILL— PARAPHRASING FOR PROBLEM SOLVING

PURPOSE

To give you practice paraphrasing thoughts and feelings.

INSTRUCTIONS

Using the situations developed in *7.9 Oral Skill—Paraphrasing for Problem Solving*, take turns paraphrasing thoughts and feelings while a classmate or your instructor uses the checklist below to evaluate you.

CHECKLIST

5 = superior   4 = excellent   3 = good   2 = fair   1 = poor

Uses appropriate nonverbal attending behaviors   _____
    —faces the speaker
    —sits upright or leans slightly toward speaker
    —looks in direction of speaker
    —facial expression indicates interest
    —vocal tone reflects interest

Asks nonleading questions as appropriate   _____

Fluently and concisely paraphrases the speaker's thoughts   _____

Fluently and concisely paraphrases the speaker's feelings   _____

Expresses paraphrasing in a tentative manner; invites verification
by the speaker verbally or nonverbally   _____

                                                  Total   _____

▲ 7.11 IDENTIFYING INFORMATIONAL PARAPHRASING RESPONSES

PURPOSE

To develop your ability to recognize paraphrasing responses.

INSTRUCTIONS

1. Identify the best paraphrasing response to each statement below.
2. Check your answers in the back of this manual on page 282.

1. Boss to employee: "Draft a letter that denies this request for a refund, but make it tactful."
   a. "What do you want me to say?"
   b. "How can I say no tactfully?"
   c. "So I should explain nicely why we can't give a refund, right?"
   d. "In other words, you want me to give this customer the brush-off?"

2. Friend says, "How do they expect us to satisfy the course requirements when there aren't enough spaces in the classes we're supposed to take?"
   a. "So you're frustrated because you can't get into the courses you need, huh?"
   b. "You think that some of the courses are worthless—is that it?"
   c. "Sounds like you're sorry you chose this major."
   d. "Why don't you write a letter to the chairperson of the department?"

3. Friend says, "Why don't I meet you after class at the student union?"
   a. "So you want me to pick you up at the student union?"
   b. "You want me to pick you up *again*?"
   c. "So we'll meet at the south entrance around 5:15?"
   d. "Why can't you drive yourself? Is your car broken again?"

4. Co-worker advises, "When you go in for a job interview, be sure and talk about the internship, your coursework, and your extracurricular activities. Don't expect them to ask you."
   a. "You think they won't ask about those things?"
   b. "Won't that sound like bragging?"
   c. "Why should I talk about the internship?"
   d. "So you're saying not to be bashful about stressing my experience?"

5. Friend says, "I don't think it's right that they go out and recruit women when there are plenty of good men around."
   a. "Sounds like you're angry because you think they're so concerned about being fair to women that they're being unfair to men, right?"
   b. "You're right—that doesn't sound fair."
   c. "If you don't think it's fair, you ought to speak up."
   d. "I can see that you're angry. What makes you think women are being given an unfair advantage?"

▲ 7.12 IDENTIFYING PARAPHRASING FOR PROBLEM SOLVING

PURPOSE

To help you identify complete and accurate paraphrasing responses to another's problem.

BACKGROUND

In order for a paraphrasing response to be most helpful, it should contain a reflection of both the speaker's *thoughts* and *feelings*.

INSTRUCTIONS

1. For each of the statements below, identify which response is the most complete and accurate reflection of the speaker's message.
2. Check your answers in the back of this manual on page 282.

1. "Sometimes I think I'd like to drop out of school, but then I start to feel like a quitter."
   a. "Maybe it would be helpful to take a break. You can always come back, you know."
   b. "You're afraid that you might fail if you stay in school now, is that it?"
   c. "I can really relate to what you're saying. I feel awkward here myself sometimes."
   d. "So you'd feel ashamed of yourself if you quit now, even though you'd like to?"

2. "I don't want to go to the party. I won't know anyone there, and I'll wind up sitting by myself all night."
   a. "You're afraid that you won't be able to approach anybody and nobody will want to talk to you?"
   b. "You never know; you could have a great time."
   c. "So you really don't want to go, eh?"
   d. "What makes you think it will be that way?"

3. "I get really nervous talking to my professor. I keep thinking that I sound stupid."
   a. "Talking to her is really a frightening experience?"
   b. "You're saying that you'd rather not approach her?"
   c. "You get the idea that she's evaluating you, and that leaves you feeling uncomfortable?"
   d. "You think that talking to her might affect your grade for the worse?"

4. "I don't know what to do about my kids. Their whining is driving me crazy."
   a. "Even though whining is natural, it's getting to you?"
   b. "Sometimes you really get fed up with their complaining?"
   c. "You're getting angry at them?"
   d. "Even the best parents get irritated sometimes."

5. "I just blew another test in that class. Why can't I do better?"
   a. "You probably need to study harder. You'll get it!"
   b. "You're feeling sorry for yourself because you've done all you can do and you still can't pull a better grade?"
   c. "Where do you think the problem is?"
   d. "You're discouraged and frustrated because you don't know what you're doing wrong?"

▲ 7.13 IDENTIFYING TYPES OF LISTENING

PURPOSE
To give you practice in identifying types of listening.

INSTRUCTIONS
1. Match the letter of the listening type with its example found below.
2. Check your answers in the back of this manual on page 282.

    a. advising   c. analyzing   e. supporting   g. paraphrasing
    b. judging   d. questioning   f. prompting

_____ 1. "So what do you mean?"

_____ 2. "You're mad at me for postponing the meeting?"

_____ 3. "You're probably just more upset than usual because of the stress of exams."

_____ 4. "What reason did she give for not attending?"

_____ 5. "Well, that was good of him not to complain."

_____ 6. "Have you tried praising her?"

_____ 7. "Have you tried talking to him about it?"

_____ 8. "Are you as excited as you sound about this big meet?"

_____ 9. "Jim should not have said that to Amy after you asked him not to."

_____ 10. "And then what happened?"

_____ 11. "So why did you go to Ellie's in the first place?"

_____ 12. "You really are good; they'll recognize that."

_____ 13. "It's not fair for you to have to work nights."

_____ 14. "Maybe you should give her a taste of her own medicine."

_____ 15. "And so you feel like retaliating because you're hurt?"

CHAPTER EIGHT

▲ INTIMACY AND DISTANCE ▲ IN RELATIONSHIPS

▲ I. INTIMACY AND DISTANCE: STRIKING A BALANCE
- A. **Dimensions of Intimacy**
    1. Physical
    2. Emotional
    3. Intellectual
- B. **Distance**
    1. Change
    2. Independence
- C. **Views of Intimacy**
    1. Historical
    2. Cultural
    3. Gender

II. PRELUDE TO INTIMACY: INTERPERSONAL ATTRACTION:
- A. **We Like People Who Are Similar to Us—Usually**
- B. **We Like People Who Are Different from Us—In Certain Ways**
- C. **We Like People Who Like Us—Usually**
- D. **We Are Attracted to People Who Can Help Us**
- E. **We Like Competent People—Particularly When They're Human**
- F. **We Are Attracted to People Who Disclose Themselves to Us—Appropriately**
- G. **We Feel Strongly about People We Encounter Often**

III. DEVELOPMENTAL STAGES IN INTIMATE RELATIONSHIPS
- A. **Stages of Coming Together and Coming Apart**
    1. Initiating
    2. Experimenting
    3. Intensifying

4. Integrating
5. Bonding
6. Differentiating
7. Circumscribing
8. Stagnating
9. Avoiding
10. Terminating

B. **Movement within and between Stages**
 1. Movement occurs within stages
 2. Movement between steps is generally sequential
 3. Relationships are constantly changing
  a. Connection and autonomy
  b. Openness and privacy
  c. Predictability and novelty
 4. Movement is always to a new place

IV. **SELF-DISCLOSURE IN RELATIONSHIPS**
 A. **Definition**
  1. Deliberate
  2. Significant
  3. Not known by others

 B. **Degrees of Self-Disclosure**
  1. Social penetration model: Breadth and depth
  2. Levels: Clichés, facts, opinions, feelings

 C. **The Johari Window Model of Self-Disclosure: Open, Hidden, Blind, Unknown**

 D. **Characteristics of Self-Disclosure**
  1. Usually occurs in dyads
  2. Occurs incrementally
  3. Few transactions involve high levels
  4. Usually occurs in positive relationships

 E. **Self-Disclosure Is Influenced by Culture**

 F. **Reasons for Self-Disclosure**
  1. Catharsis
  2. Self-clarification
  3. Self-validation
  4. Reciprocity
  5. Impression formation
  6. Relationship maintenance and enhancement
  7. Social control
  8. Manipulation

 G. **Guidelines for Self-Disclosure**
  1. Consider the importance of the other person
  2. Evaluate the risks involved
  3. Make the amount and type of self-disclosure appropriate
  4. Make the disclosure relevant to the situation at hand
  5. Reciprocate disclosure as appropriate

6. Consider constructive effects
7. Make the disclosure clear and understandable

V. ALTERNATIVES TO SELF-DISCLOSURE

A. Lies
1. White lies
2. Reasons for lying
   a. Save face
   b. Avoid tension/conflict
   c. Guide social interaction
   d. Expand/reduce relationships
   e. Gain power
3. Effects of lies

B. Equivocation

C. The Ethics of Evasion

▲ KEY TERMS

attraction variables
avoiding
bonding
breadth
catharsis
circumscribing
clichés
depth
differentiating
equivocal language
exchange theory
experimenting
facts
feelings
impression formation
initiating
integrating
intensifying

intimacy
Johari Window
lie
manipulation
opinions
reciprocity
relational enhancement
self-clarification
self-disclosure
self-validation
small talk
social control
social penetration
stages of relationships
stagnating
terminating
uncertainty reduction
white lie

▲ 8.1 ATTRACTION VARIABLES

PURPOSE

To identify the attraction variables that led to your relationship with two persons important to you.

INSTRUCTIONS

1. Identify two people who are not blood relatives with whom you have important relationships. Briefly describe the relationship of Person A and Person B below.
2. Comment on each of the attraction variables listed below for each relationship. Describe how that variable did or did not play a role in the development of your relationship.

Attraction Variable	Person A Relationship	Person B Relationship
1. We are similar to one another.		
2. We are different from one another—in complementary ways.		
3. We like one another.		
4. We help one another.		

Attraction Variable	Person A Relationship	Person B Relationship
5. We view one another as competent but human.		
6. We engage in appropriate self-disclosure.		
7. We see one another frequently.		

Summarize the ways you are attracted to others. What types of relationships require what types of attraction as far as you are concerned? Describe the differences in attraction for romantic relationships versus friendships or professional relationships.

_____

_____

_____

_____

_____

_____

▲ 8.2 DEFINING STAGES IN RELATIONSHIPS

PURPOSES

1. To identify the stages in your interpersonal relationships.
2. To describe the behaviors that characterize the stages of your relationships.
3. To suggest ways of controlling the direction of your relationships.

INSTRUCTIONS

1. Describe two relationships you have with different persons. Give enough background information to explain how you arrived at the stage you'll explain in 2 and 3 below. Pick two different *types* of relationships (new/old, friend, romantic interest, family, work, etc.).
2. At which stage do you think your relationship is at the present time?

initiating	differentiating
experimenting	circumscribing
intensifying	stagnating
integrating	avoiding
bonding	terminating

3. Describe your behaviors and those of your partner in the relationship that reflect this stage and tend to define the relationship at this stage. Be sure you give enough examples of behavior to justify your claim that the two of you are in or between certain stages.
4. Describe the direction you think the relationship will take. Describe your satisfaction or dissatisfaction with this direction and what you might do to control the direction the relationship takes.

EXAMPLE

1. Person and relationship *My friend Sue and I met in a class at school nine years ago, and we've also been together in social contexts, in religious ones (we belong to the same church, it turned out), and in some neighborhood ones (she moved closer to me a few years ago). We've spent many hours telling one another personal information that involves intellectual and emotional intimacy, and we've had a lot of fun together. We have a history of doing big favors for one another, and our social circles merged over the years.*
2. Stage *I think Sue and I are in the differentiating stage in our relationship now.*
3. Behaviors reflecting the stage *After Sue went through a painful divorce last year, and a lot of loneliness that followed, she decided to move away from here to return to the area where she has a lot of family; I find myself finding differences between us, where once I found only similarities—I've started talking more about "me" and so has Sue, whereas we once talked almost exclusively about "we." We both are putting some distance in our relationship—not visiting as often, not calling as much, talking about individual interests, and talking about our futures separately. We still reaffirm our "lifelong" friendship, but we realize we're not willing to give up everything for one another.*
4. Direction/satisfaction *I think our relationship will get a little more distant for a while. We may even circumscribe a bit, talking about everything else in our lives except the level of our own commitment to one another. I think we will probably stabilize at the intensifying stage in the many times we will come together again (and in our many long telephone conversations). The distance*

between us and the little physical time we'll spend together will make us less intimate. I know Sue will always be my superb friend, but in a different way than in the past. I'm not satisfied that this relationship will allow distance to separate us, but there is not much I think I can do to change it. I will call, and I will visit, but it will never be the same as it has been because we just won't be able to share all the things we have in the past, and we both will probably change in different directions without being able to understand as well as when we saw one another and talked every day. But I think we will always want to call the other with that "special" information, and we'll laugh and cry together because we have such a base for friendship with all we've shared. The relationship will be defined differently than in the past, and I think I can be satisfied with that.

RELATIONSHIP A

1. Person and relationship

_____

_____

_____

_____

_____

_____

_____

_____

_____

_____

_____

_____

2. Stage _____

_____

3. **Behaviors reflecting the stage**

_____

_____

_____

_____

_____

4. **Direction/satisfaction**

_____

_____

_____

_____

_____

RELATIONSHIP B

1. **Person and relationship**

_____

_____

_____

_____

_____

_____

_____

_____

_____

_____

_____

_____

_____

_____

2. Stage _____

_____

3. Behaviors reflecting the stage

_____

_____

_____

_____

4. Direction/satisfaction

_____

_____

_____

_____

_____

_____

_____

▲ 8.3 BREADTH AND DEPTH OF RELATIONSHIPS

PURPOSES

1. To help you understand the breadth and depth of a relationship that is important to you.
2. To help you decide if you are satisfied with the breadth and depth of that relationship, and possibly to modify it.

INSTRUCTIONS

1. Use the form below to make a social penetration model for a significant relationship you have, indicating the depth and breadth of various areas. See Figure 8.1 and 8.2 in Chapter 8 of *Looking Out/Looking In* for an example of the social penetration model.
2. Answer the questions at the end of the exercise.

SOCIAL PENETRATION MODEL

Significant relationship described:

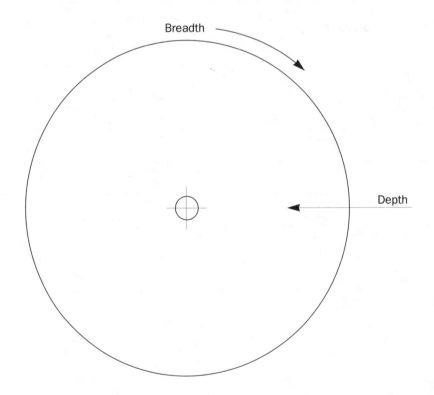

CONCLUSIONS

How deep or hallow is your relationship with this person?

_____

_____

Does the depth vary from one area (breadth) to another? In what way?

_____

_____

_____

Are you satisfied with the depth and breadth of this relationship?

_____

_____

_____

What could you do to change the relationship?

_____

_____

_____

_____

_____

_____

_____

▲ 8.4 REASONS FOR NONDISCLOSURE*

PURPOSE

To give you an idea of the reasons you do not disclose and the rationality of these reasons.

INSTRUCTIONS

1. Choose a particular individual about whom you want to analyze your self-disclosing behavior.
2. In the column to the left of each item, indicate the extent to which you use each reason to avoid disclosing.

       5 = almost always   2 = rarely
       4 = often   1 = never
       3 = sometimes

3. In the column to the right of each item, indicate how reasonable and realistic the reason is.

       5 = totally realistic
       4 = mostly realistic
       3 = partially realistic, partly unrealistic
       2 = mostly unrealistic
       1 = totally unrealistic

How Frequently Do You Use the Reason?   **How Realistic and Rational Is the Reason?**

How Frequently Do You Use the Reason?		How Realistic and Rational Is the Reason?
_____	1. I can't find the opportunity to self-disclose with this person.	_____
_____	2. If I disclose I might hurt the other person.	_____
_____	3. If I disclose I might be evaluating or judging the person.	_____
_____	4. I can't think of topics that I would disclose.	_____
_____	5. Self-disclosure would give information that might be used against me at some time.	_____
_____	6. If I disclose it might cause me to make personal changes.	_____
_____	7. Self-disclosure might threaten relationships I have with people other than the close acquaintance to whom I disclose.	_____
_____	8. Self-disclosure is a sign of weakness.	_____
_____	9. If I disclose I might lose control over the other person.	_____
_____	10. If I disclose I might discover I am less than I wish to be.	_____

*Based on a survey developed by Lawrence B. Rosenfeld, "Self-Disclosure Avoidance: Why Am I Afraid to Tell You Who I Am?," *Communication Monographs* 46 (1979): 63–74.

**How Frequently
Do You Use
the Reason?**

**How Realistic
and Rational
Is the Reason?**

_____   11. If I disclose I might project an image I do not want to project.   _____

_____   12. If I disclose the other person might not understand what I
was saying.   _____

_____   13. If I disclose the other person might evaluate me negatively.   _____

_____   14. Self-disclosure is a sign of some emotional disturbance.   _____

_____   15. Self-disclosure might hurt our relationship.   _____

_____   16. I am afraid that self-disclosure might lead to an intimate
relationship with the other person.   _____

_____   17. Self-disclosure might threaten my physical safety.   _____

_____   18. If I disclose I might give information that makes me
appear inconsistent.   _____

_____   19. Any other reasons: _____   _____

_____

What does this personal survey tell you about your thoughts and feelings about self-disclosure
with this person?

_____

_____

_____

_____

Do you think your level of self-disclosure is appropriate or inappropriate with this person? Why?

_____

_____

_____

▲ 8.5 DEGREES OF SELF-DISCLOSURE

PURPOSES

1. To demonstrate that self-disclosure can operate on a variety of levels, some quite intimate and others less revealing.
2. To give you practice in applying various types of self-disclosure to personal situations.

INSTRUCTIONS

For each of the following topics, write two statements for each level of self-disclosure. (See Chapter 8 of *Looking Out/Looking In* for descriptions of each level.)

EXAMPLE

Topic: School

1. Clichés
    a. *These exams are sure a drag!*
    b. *Textbooks are sure expensive!*

2. Facts
    a. *I'm a psychology major at the University of Oregon.*
    b. *I'm getting a teaching certificate so I'll be able to teach social studies.*

3. Opinions
    a. *I believe in affirmative action but I don't think there should be quotas for women and minorities.*
    b. *I don't think instructors should count class participation as part of a person's grade.*

4. Feelings
    a. *I feel scared when I think about the future. I'm almost finished with four years of college, and I'm still confused about what to do with my life.*
    b. *I get angry when Professor Autel doesn't prepare for our class.*

TOPIC: MY FAMILY

1. Clichés

    a. _____

    b. _____

2. Facts

    a. _____

    b. _____

3. Opinions

   a. _____

   b. _____

4. Feelings

   a. _____

   b. _____

TOPIC: MY CAREER PLANS

1. Clichés

   a. _____

   b. _____

2. Facts

   a. _____

   b. _____

3. Opinions

   a. _____

   b. _____

4. Feelings

   a. _____

   b. _____

TOPIC: MY FRIENDSHIPS

1. Clichés

   a. _____

   b. _____

2. Facts

    a. _____

    b. _____

3. Opinions

    a. _____

    b. _____

4. Feelings

    a. _____

    b. _____

TOPIC: SPORTS

1. Clichés

    a. _____

    b. _____

2. Facts

    a. _____

    b. _____

3. Opinions

    a. _____

    b. _____

4. Feelings

    a. _____

    b. _____

NAME _____

▲ 8.6 SELF-DISCLOSURE DIARY

PURPOSE

To help you discover how much and what types of self-disclosure you engage in.

INSTRUCTIONS

1. Use the space below to monitor your self-disclosure with one important person over the course of a day, evening, weekend, or any period of time in which you'll interact with some frequency. Describe at least three different situations.
2. In the **Conclusions** section of this exercise, estimate the percentages of each level of self-disclosure you use with this important person, discuss your patterns of self-disclosure, and establish a self-disclosure goal for the relationship.

EXAMPLE

Jean, my friend

Situation *While running together*

Cliché statements: *"Boy, some days running's really hard."*

Fact statements: *"I had a fight with Chris today." "Finals start in two weeks." "I bought a VCR."*

Opinion statements: *"I think that schools ought to emphasize fitness more than they do." "I don't think people should go into teaching unless they really love kids."*

Feeling statements: *"I sure enjoy our time together." "I feel angry and hurt that Rick didn't return my call."*

Notice that this example includes cliche, fact, opinion, and feeling statements. This was done to clarify the characteristics of each type of disclosure. It is quite possible that in your own monitoring you will discover more of one type than another.

Situation 1: _____

Types of self-disclosure statements I usually make: _____

Behavioral examples (quotes, descriptions): _____

_____

_____

Types of self-disclosure statements partner usually makes: _____

Behavioral examples (quotes, descriptions): _____

_____

_____

Situation 2: _____

Types of self-disclosure statements I usually make: _____

Behavioral examples (quotes, descriptions): _____

_____

_____

Types of self-disclosure statements partner usually makes: _____

Behavioral examples (quotes, descriptions): _____

_____

_____

Situation 3: _____

Types of self-disclosure statements I usually make: _____

Behavioral examples (quotes, descriptions): _____

_____

_____

Types of self-disclosure statements partner usually makes: _____

Behavioral examples (quotes, descriptions): _____

_____

_____

CONCLUSIONS

Now review the information you recorded and describe the self-disclosure patterns you have observed. Then establish a clear goal for the relationship.

Sample self-disclosure pattern *Most of our conversations involved facts and opinions, with very few clichés and almost no feelings expressed.*

Goal *During the next week I will disclose at least two feeling statements to my friend. Specifically, I will describe my feelings of excitement and apprehension about my new job. I will also tell her how secure and supported I feel in my relationship with her.*

Self-disclosure patterns _____

_____

_____

_____

_____

How satisfactory is this to you? _____

_____

_____

Goal (What would you do to change?) _____

_____

_____

_____

_____

▲ 8.7 ALTERNATIVES TO SELF-DISCLOSURE

PURPOSES

1. To consider the responsible alternatives to self-disclosure in a given situation.
2. To generate possible responses.
3. To identify the functions served by these responses.
4. To evaluate the ethics of evading self-disclosure.

INSTRUCTIONS

1. Using the situations described below, record your responses. They may be full disclosure, partial disclosure, white lies, or equivocation.
2. Identify the response and its function in the relationship as in the following examples:
    White lie: save face, avoid tension/conflict, guide social interaction, expand/reduce relationships, gain power
    Equivocation: a function listed above or desire for keeping situation open
3. Evaluate the ethics of your response.

EXAMPLE

Your friend asks you if you had a good time when you went out with his cousin last night.

Response *"Yeah, your cousin was a lot of fun and the movie was great." (The movie was OK, but his cousin was a real bore.)*

Type/Function *This white lie basically lets me avoid tension in the relationship with my friend.*

Ethics of response *While I haven't been truthful with my friend, I just don't want to tell him how boring I think his cousin is. I think it is better to just be nice to him and his cousin. Then both of them can save face, too.*

1. Your parent calls and asks how you are doing in classes. You don't think you're doing as well as he/she would like you to.

    Response _____

    _____

    _____

    Type/Function _____

    _____

    _____

Ethics _____

_____

_____

_____

_____

2. Your professor asks how you are enjoying the class so far. You're not sure how the professor would react no matter what you say.

Response _____

_____

_____

Type/Function _____

_____

_____

Ethics _____

_____

_____

_____

_____

3. A co-worker asks how you like the job you've just started. You're not sure about your feelings yet.

Response _____

_____

_____

Type/Function _____

_____

_____

Ethics _____

_____

_____

_____

_____

4. Your roommates ask what you think of the bright posters they've just put up around the room. You think they're a bit tacky.

Response _____

_____

_____

Type/Function _____

_____

_____

Ethics _____

_____

_____

_____

5. Your romantic partner asks how many other people you've really loved before you met him/her. You don't want to be truthful.

Response _____

_____

_____

Type/Function _____

_____

_____

Ethics _____

_____

_____

_____

_____

6. Your very opinionated father asks what you think of the people running for political office. You disagree with his views.

Response _____

_____

_____

Type/Function _____

_____

_____

Ethics _____

_____

_____

_____

_____

7. Your boss at work wants to know what your plans for the future are. You plan to leave as soon as you find a better job.

Response _____

_____

_____

Type/Function _____

_____

_____

Ethics _____

_____

_____

_____

_____

8. Your mother asks you about what your brother/sister has been up to lately. They have been doing something she wouldn't be happy to hear.

Response _____

_____

_____

Type/Function _____

_____

_____

Ethics _____

_____

_____

_____

_____

9. Your romantic partner wants to know why you are spending so much time with your other friends. You've been bored with the relationship lately.

Response _____

_____

_____

Type/Function _____

_____

_____

Ethics _____

_____

_____

_____

_____

▲ 8.8 ORAL SKILL—
ILLUSTRATING APPROPRIATE SELF-DISCLOSURE

PURPOSES

1. To illustrate different degrees of self-disclosure.
2. To illustrate alternatives to self-disclosure.
3. To help develop self-disclosure behaviors with which you are comfortable.

INSTRUCTIONS

1. With a partner discuss the various situations listed below. Either pick a situation with which you can identify, or generate a situation of your own and clear it with your instructor.
2. Develop a role-play surrounding the situations you find below (or demonstrate a real-life situation you have generated) that illustrates various levels of self-disclosure from both parties (cliché, fact, opinion, feeling).
   Or
   Illustrate self-disclosure from one partner followed by the alternatives to self-disclosure (white lie, equivocation).
   Or
   Demonstrate various levels of self-disclosure and explain which level you think is best.
3. After your role-play, identify the levels and/or alternatives. Justify your self-disclosure levels in light of the ethics of evasion and the demands of the relationship.

OPTION:

Videotape your role-play, play it for the class, and identify your levels and alternatives as you stop and start the tape.

SELF-DISCLOSURE SITUATIONS:

1. Friends are telling one another about their use of/refusal to use drugs.
2. Two classmates are comparing their grades.
3. A boyfriend and girlfriend are telling one another about their past romantic involvements.
4. Two friends are shopping for clothes and giving one another advice on what looks good/bad.
5. A parent asks a 20-year-old about his/her weekend.
6. A manager and employee have agreed to sit down and talk about the problems they are experiencing with one another.
7. A friend has just experienced a death in the family and the partner is expressing concern.
8. Two acquaintances are exchanging their attitudes toward marriage.
9. Two women are discussing child bearing.
10. Two friends are discussing their worries and feelings of responsibility regarding their parents getting older.
11. Two friends are discussing the effects of divorce in their families.

▲ 8.9 CHECKLIST FOR ORAL SKILL — ILLUSTRATING SELF-DISCLOSURE

PURPOSES

1. To illustrate different levels of self-disclosure.
2. To illustrate alternatives to self-disclosure.
3. To describe behavioral choices involved in self-disclosure.

INSTRUCTIONS

1. Using the role-plays developed in *8.8 Oral Skill—Illustrating Appropriate Self-Disclosure*, illustrate conversations involving self-disclosure and/or alternatives to self-disclosure.
2. Identify the levels and/or alternatives.
3. Justify your behaviors in light of the relationship.

CHECKLIST

5 = superior   4 = excellent   3 = good   2 = fair   1 = poor

Uses appropriate nonverbal attending behaviors   _____
 —looks in the direction of the other
 —uses appropriate tone of voice
 —leans slightly toward other as appropriate
 —uses facial expression appropriate to the self-disclosure
 —uses voice and expression appropriate to the self-disclosure alternative

Illustrates levels of self-disclosure

Illustrates alternatives to self-disclosure   _____

Identifies levels of self-disclosure correctly   _____

Identifies alternatives to self-disclosure   _____

Justifies self-disclosure/alternatives in light of the relationship   _____

               Total   _____

▲ 8.10 IDENTIFYING DEVELOPMENTAL STAGES

PURPOSE

To give you practice in identifying developmental stages in intimate relationships.

INSTRUCTIONS

1. Match the letter of the developmental stage with its description found below.
2. Check your answers in the back of this manual on page 282.

Place the letter of the developmental stage of the intimate relationships on the line before its example found below.

a.	initiating	f.	differentiating
b.	experimenting	g.	circumscribing
c.	intensifying	h.	stagnating
d.	integrating	i.	avoiding
e.	bonding	j.	terminating

_____ 1. A public ritual marks this stage.

_____ 2. First glances and "sizing up" one another typifies this stage.

_____ 3. Called the "we" stage, this stage involves increasing self-disclosure.

_____ 4. Lots of "small talk" typifies this stage.

_____ 5. This stage involves much focus on individual rather than dyadic interests.

_____ 6. There's very little growth or experimentation in this stage.

_____ 7. This stage involves much behavior that talks around the relational issues because the partners expect bad feelings.

_____ 8. The partners' social circles merge at this stage and they make purchases or commitments together.

_____ 9. No attempts are made to contact the other at this stage.

_____ 10. The relationship is redefined or dissolved at this stage.

▲ IMPROVING COMMUNICATION ▲
CLIMATES

▲ **I. COMMUNICATION CLIMATE: THE KEY TO POSITIVE RELATIONSHIPS**
   A. Confirming Communication
      1. Recognition
      2. Acknowledgement
      3. Endorsement
   B. Discomforting Communication
      1. Verbal abuse
      2. Complaining
      3. Impervious
      4. Interrupting
      5. Irrelevant
      6. Tangential
      7. Impersonal
      8. Ambiguous
      9. Incongruous
   C. How Communication Climates Develop
      1. Escalatory conflict spirals
      2. Deescalatory conflict spirals

 II. DEFENSIVENESS: CAUSES AND REMEDIES
   A. Causes
   B. Types of Defensive Reactions
      1. Attacking the critic
         a. Verbal aggression
         b. Sarcasm
      2. Distorting critical information
         a. Rationalization
         b. Compensation
         c. Regression

3. Avoiding dissonant information
    a. Physical avoidance
    b. Repression
    c. Apathy
    d. Displacement

C. **Preventing Defensiveness in Others**
    1. Evaluation vs. description
    2. Control vs. problem orientation
    3. Strategy vs. spontaneity
    4. Neutrality vs. empathy
    5. Superiority vs. equality
    6. Certainty vs. provisionalism

D. **Responding Nondefensively to Criticism**
    1. Seek more information
        a. Ask for specifics
        b. Guess about specifics
        c. Paraphrase the speaker's ideas
        d. Ask what the critic wants
        e. Ask about the consequences of your behavior
        f. Ask what else is wrong
    2. Agree with the critic
        a. Agree with the truth
        b. Agree with the critic's perception

▲ KEY TERMS

acknowledgment
ambiguous response
apathy
certainty
cognitive dissonance
communication climate
compensation
complaining
cognitive dissonance
confirming communication
controlling communication
criticism
deescalatory conflict spirals
defense mechanism
defensiveness
descriptive communication
discomforting communication
displacement
empathy
endorsement
equality
escalatory conflict spirals
evaluative communication
face-threatening act

Gibb categories
impersonal response
impervious response
incongruous response
indifference
interrupting response
irrelevant response
neutrality
physical avoidance
problem orientation
provisionalism
rationalization
recognition
regression
repression
sarcasm
spiral
spontaneity
strategy
superiority
tangential response
verbal abuse
verbal aggression

▲ 9.1 UNDERSTANDING YOUR DEFENSIVE RESPONSES

PURPOSE

To help you identify your typical defensive responses.

INSTRUCTIONS

1. Identify the person or people who would be most likely to deliver each of the following critical messages to you. If you are unlikely to hear one or more of the following messages, substitute a defensiveness-arousing topic of your own.
2. For each situation, describe
    a. the person likely to deliver the message
    b. the typical content of the message
    c. the general type of response(s) you make: attacking, distorting, or avoiding
    d. your typical verbal response(s)
    e. your typical nonverbal response(s)
    f. the part of your presenting self being defended
    g. the probable consequences of these response(s)

EXAMPLE

A negative comment about your use of time.

Person likely to deliver this message *my parents*

Typical content of the message *wasting my time watching TV instead of studying*

General type(s) of response *attacking, distorting*

Your typical verbal response(s) *"Get off my back! I work hard! I need time to relax." "I'll study later; I've got plenty of time."*

Your typical nonverbal response(s) *harsh tone of voice, sullen silence for an hour or two*

Part of presenting self being defended *good student, not lazy*

Probable consequences of your response(s) *uncomfortable silence, more criticism from parents in the future*

1. Negative comment about your appearance.

    Person likely to deliver this message _____

    Typical content of the message _____

    _____

    General type(s) of response _____

Your typical verbal response(s) _____

_____

Your typical nonverbal response(s) _____

_____

2. Criticism about your choice of friends.

   Person likely to deliver this message _____

   Typical content of the message _____

   _____

   General type(s) of response _____

   Your typical verbal response(s) _____

   _____

   Your typical nonverbal response(s) _____

   _____

   Part(s) of presenting self being defended _____

   Probable consequences of your response(s) _____

   _____

   _____

3. Criticism of a job you've just completed.

   Person likely to deliver this message _____

   Typical content of the message _____

   _____

   General type(s) of response _____

   Your typical verbal response(s) _____

   _____

Your typical nonverbal response(s) _____

_____

Part(s) of presenting self being defended _____

Probable consequences of your response(s) _____

_____

_____

4. Criticism of your schoolwork.

   Person likely to deliver this message _____

   Typical content of the message _____

   _____

   General type(s) of response _____

   Your typical verbal response(s) _____

   _____

   Your typical nonverbal response(s) _____

   _____

   Part(s) of presenting self being defended _____

   Probable consequences of your response(s) _____

   _____

   _____

5. Criticism of your diet or eating habits.

   Person likely to deliver this message _____

   Typical content of the message _____

   _____

   General type(s) of response _____

Your typical verbal response(s) _____

_____

Your typical nonverbal response(s) _____

_____

Part(s) of presenting self being defended _____

Probable consequences of your response(s) _____

_____

_____

6. A negative comment about your exercise (or lack of it).

Person likely to deliver this message _____

Typical content of the message _____

_____

General type(s) of response _____

Your typical verbal response(s) _____

_____

Your typical nonverbal response(s) _____

_____

Part(s) of presenting self being defended _____

Probable consequences of your response(s) _____

_____

_____

▲ 9.2 DEFENSIVE AND SUPPORTIVE LANGUAGE

PURPOSE

To help you recognize the difference between the Gibb categories of defensive and supportive language.

INSTRUCTIONS

1. For each of the situations below, write two statements a speaker might make. One should contain evaluative language and the other descriptive language.
2. In the space adjacent to each statement, label the Gibb categories of language which your words represent.

EXAMPLE

A neighbor's late-night stereo music playing is disrupting your sleep.

Defense-arousing statement *Why don't you show a little consideration and turn that damn thing down? If I hear any more noise I'm going to call the police!*

Type(s) of defensive language *evaluation, control*

Supportive statement *When I hear your stereo music late at night I can't sleep, which leaves me more and more tired. I'd like to figure out some way you can listen and I can sleep.*

Type(s) of supportive language *description, problem orientation*

1. It is two o'clock in the morning, and the parents of a teenager have been waiting up for the arrival of their son or daughter, who was expected home by midnight.

    Defense-arousing statement _____

    _____

    _____

    _____

    Type(s) of defensive language _____

    Supportive statement _____

    _____

    _____

    _____

    Type(s) of supportive language _____

2. You and your roommate split the cost of groceries and share food. Recently, however, your roommate has been bringing guests over and feasting on your food supply.

Defense-arousing statement _____

_____

_____

_____

Type(s) of defensive language _____

Supportive statement _____

_____

_____

_____

Type(s) of supportive language _____

3. A boss criticizes an employee for being late to work. The employee explains that s/he has been having car trouble.

Defense-arousing statement _____

_____

_____

_____

Type(s) of defensive language _____

Supportive statement _____

_____

_____

_____

Type(s) of supportive language _____

4. A teacher is explaining the Gibb categories to a student who is having difficulty understanding them.

Defense-arousing statement _____

_____

_____

_____

Type(s) of defensive language _____

Supportive statement _____

_____

_____

_____

Type(s) of supportive language _____

5. Two people are debating whether or not capital punishment is an appropriate means of preventing serious crimes.

Defense-arousing statement _____

_____

_____

_____

Type(s) of defensive language _____

Supportive statement _____

_____

_____

_____

Type(s) of supportive language _____

6. On many occasions a friend drops by your place without calling first. Since you often have other plans, this behavior puts you in an uncomfortable position.

Defense-arousing statement _____

_____

_____

_____

Type(s) of defensive language _____

Supportive statement _____

_____

_____

_____

Type(s) of supportive language _____

NAME _____

▲ 9.3 JOURNAL OF GIBB CATEGORIES

PURPOSES

1. To help you identify the defense-arousing and defense-reducing behaviors you use.
2. To describe defense-reducing behaviors that are alternatives to the defense-arousing ones you presently use.

INSTRUCTIONS

1. For the next several days keep track of the defense-arousing and defense-reducing behaviors you use. Use additional sheets of paper as necessary to record your behavior.
2. Identify the Gibb category of defensive or supportive behavior you used in each situation.
3. Describe the part of the self-concept that was under attack in each defense-arousing situation. (See Chapter 2 of *Looking Out/Looking In* and *2.3 Self-Concept Inventory* in this manual for example of these self-concept elements.)
4. Describe the consequences of your communication behavior in each situation.
5. For defense-arousing behaviors, describe the supportive alternative you could have used. For supportive behaviors, describe what might have happened if you had behaved in a defense-arousing manner.

Circumstances (Who Involved, Subject)	Your Behavior	Gibb Category Used	Self-Concept You Were Attacking/Supporting	Consequences	Defensive-Supportive Alternative
Example I was explaining the rules of a card game to a friend.	I said, "Come on and think" when my friend didn't understand.	Superiority, evaluation	Intelligence	My friend said, "Forget it" and stopped trying to learn.	I could have used equality and problem orientation by saying, "It's been a few years since I learned this game; help me figure out what you don't understand."
Example My uncle was complaining about "stupid" courses offered in college these days.	I listened attentively and sincerely asked questions (even though I disagreed).	Empathy, provisionalism	Credible "social observer and commentator"	My uncle's arguments didn't change my opinion, but instead of arguing we were able to spend a civil evening together and enjoy ourselves on other topics.	I could have used evaluation and superiority and said, "Well, you never finished college anyway, so who are you to comment"? We would have ended up arguing about college courses and one another, as well.

Circumstances (Who Involved, Subject)	Your Behavior	Gibb Category Used	Self-Concept You Were Attacking/Supporting	Consequences	Defensive—Supportive Alternative

▲ 9.4 COMMUNICATION CLIMATE INTERVIEW

PURPOSE

To help you understand the ways in which you help create either a defensive or supportive climate in an important relationship.

INSTRUCTIONS

1. Choose a person with whom you have an important relationship: co-worker, family member, roommate, friend, etc.
2. Explain the Gibb categories to him/her. Be a teacher yourself, and make sure your partner understands each category.
3. After finishing your explanation, ask your partner to explain which of the Gibb behaviors *you* use with him/her. Get examples to clarify this explanation: Do you use a particular behavior when a certain subject comes up? When you're in a certain mood? When your partner acts in a certain way? At a certain time?
4. Categorize your behaviors as supportive (confirming) or defensive (disconfirming). Describe each behavior and the situation in which it occurs.
5. Answer the questions at the end of the exercise.
6. When you have completed this exercise, have your partner sign it to signify that the information you recorded was accurate.

Your name _____

Name of your partner _____

Your relationship to partner _____

Partner's signature (to confirm accuracy of following information) _____

Supportive (Confirming) Behaviors Partner Reports I Use	Situations in Which I Use Each Behavior

CONCLUSIONS

Use the space below to describe how you could behave in a more confirming way with your partner in this exercise and with other people. Cite specific situations and describe specific behaviors in which you could use more confirming types of communication.

_____

_____

_____

_____

_____

_____

_____

_____

▲ 9.5 CHECKLIST FOR ORAL SKILL— SUPPORTIVE LANGUAGE EVALUATION

PURPOSE

To illustrate supportive language.

INSTRUCTIONS

1. Form foursomes. Choose two situations from *9.2 Defensive and Supportive Language* to role-play in extended form. Designate persons A, B, C, and D.
2. Persons A and B role-play one situation while C and D evaluate them using the oral skill check form for Gibb categories.
3. Persons C and D then role-play the other situation while A and B evaluate them.

OPTION:

Using Exercise *9.4 Communication Climate Interview* as a starting point, consider a situation from your life in which you would like to improve the communication climate in a relationship. Ask someone from class to role-play your real-life partner. You illustrate supportive language.

CHECKLIST

5 = superior   4 = excellent   3 = good   2 = fair   1 = poor

	Person _____	Person _____
Uses appropriate nonverbal attending behaviors		
—facial expression indicates interest in speaker	_____	_____
—vocal tone reflects sincere interest in speaker	_____	_____
—maintains appropriate amount of eye contact comfortable to both speakers	_____	_____
—faces partner while talking and listening	_____	_____
Uses supportive language as appropriate		
—description	_____	_____
—problem orientation	_____	_____
—spontaneity	_____	_____
—empathy	_____	_____
—equality	_____	_____
—provisionalism	_____	_____
Copes effectively with criticism as needed	_____	_____
Total	_____	_____

▲ 9.6 COPING WITH TYPICAL CRITICISM

PURPOSE

To help you practice nondefensive responses to typical criticisms you face.

INSTRUCTIONS

OPTION A:

1. For each situation below, write a nondefensive response you could use that follows the guidelines of seeking more information and/or agreeing with the critic described in Chapter 9 of *Looking Out/Looking In*.
2. Join with two partners and identify the members as A, B, and C.
3. Role-play situations 1 and 2 with A responding to the criticisms offered by B, while C uses *9.5 Checklist for Oral Skill —Supportive Language Evaluation* to evaluate A's behavior.
4. Switch roles so that B responds to C's criticisms on items 3 and 4, while A completes the checklist.
5. Switch roles again so that C responds to A's criticisms on items 5 and 6, while B completes the checklist.

OPTION B:

1. Form triads and identify members as A, B, and C.
2. Person A describes a common defensiveness-arousing criticism s/he faces, identifying the critic, topic, and the critic's behavior.
3. Person B paraphrases and questions A until s/he understands the critic's behavior.
4. Persons A and B then role-play the situation, with A practicing the skills of seeking more information and agreeing with the critic as described in Chapter 9 of *Looking Out/Looking In*.
5. Person C uses *9.7 Checklist for Oral Skill —Coping With Typical Criticism* to evaluate A's skill at responding nondefensively.
6. After the role-play, person C provides feedback to person A.
7. Rotate roles and repeat steps 1–6 until both B and C have had the chance to practice responding nondefensively to criticism.

OPTION C:

Videotape your coping with the criticism of a partner for later evaluation.

Situation	How I Could Respond Effectively to This Criticism
1. You've been late to work every day this week. Just who do you think you are that you can come wandering in after the rest of us are already working?	

Situation	How I Could Respond Effectively to This Criticism
2. This place is a mess! Don't you care about how we live?	
3. No wonder your grades are low. You're always out partying instead of studying.	
4. How could you have been so thoughtless at the party last night?	
5. You think I'm your personal servant!	
6. What's the matter with you? You've been so cold lately.	
7. Your motivation level sure is low lately.	

▲ 9.7 CHECKLIST FOR ORAL SKILL—COPING WITH TYPICAL CRITICISM

CHECKLIST

5 = superior   4 = excellent   3 = good   2 = fair   1 = poor

Seeks additional information to understand criticism and critic

   —asks for specific details of criticism   _____

   —guesses about specific details when critic does not supply facts   _____

   —paraphrases critic to clarify criticism and draw out more information   _____

   —asks what the critic wants   _____

   —asks critic to describe the consequences of behavior ("How does my behavior cause problems for you?")   _____

   —asks what else is wrong   _____

Agrees as appropriate with criticism

   —agrees with facts (truth only)   _____

   —agrees with critic's right to perceive event differently ("I can understand why it looks that way to you because . . .")   _____

Maintains appropriate nonverbal behaviors to indicate sincerity   _____
   —voice
   —facial expression
   —posture and gestures
   —body orientation and distance

                       Total   _____

▲ 9.8 IDENTIFYING DEFENSIVENESS AND SUPPORTIVENESS

PURPOSE

To give you practice in identifying defensive and supportive behaviors.

INSTRUCTIONS

1. Match the letter of the defensive or supportive category with its description of behavior found below.
2. Check your answers in the back of this manual on page 282.

a.	evaluation	g.	description
b.	control	h.	problem orientation
c.	strategy	i.	spontaneity
d.	neutrality	j.	empathy
e.	superiority	k.	equality
f.	certainty	l.	provisionalism

_____ 1. Gerry insists he has all the facts and needs to hear no more information.

_____ 2. Richard has a strong opinion but will listen to another position.

_____ 3. Lina kept looking at the clock as she was listening to Nan, so Nan thought Lina didn't consider her comments as very important.

_____ 4. "I know Janice doesn't agree with me," Mary said, "but she knows how strongly I feel about this, and I think she understands my position."

_____ 5. "Even though my professor has a Ph.D.," Rosa pointed out, "she doesn't act like she's the only one who knows something; she is really interested in me as a person."

_____ 6. "When I found out that Bob had tricked me into thinking his proposal was my idea so I'd support it, I was really angry."

_____ 7. "Even though we **all** wait tables here, Evanne thinks she's better than any of us—just look at the way she prances around!"

_____ 8. Clara sincerely and honestly told Georgia about her reservations concerning Georgia's planned party.

_____ 9. The co-workers attempted to find a solution to the scheduling issue that would satisfy both of their needs.

_____ 10. "It seems as though my father's favorite phrase is `I know what's best for you' and that really gripes me."

_____ 11. "You drink too much."

_____ 12. "I was embarrassed when you slurred your speech in front of my boss."

_____ 13. "The flowers and presents are just an attempt to get me to go to bed with him."

_____ 14. "She looked down her nose at me when I told her I didn't exercise regularly."

_____ 15. "Well, if you need more money and I need more help around here, what could we do to make us both happy?"

CHAPTER TEN

▲ MANAGING INTERPERSONAL CONFLICTS ▲

▲ **I. THE NATURE OF CONFLICT**
  A. **Definition**
    1. Expressed struggle
    2. Perceived incompatible goals
    3. Perceived scarce rewards
  B. **Conflict Is Natural**
  C. **Conflict Can Be Beneficial**

II. PERSONAL CONFLICT STYLES
  A. **Nonassertive Behavior**
    1. Avoidance
    2. Accommodation
  B. **Direct Aggression**
  C. **Passive Aggression—Crazymaking**
  D. **Indirect Communication**
  E. **Assertion**
  F. **Determining the Best Style**
    1. Situation
    2. Receiver
    3. Your goals

III. ASSERTION WITHOUT AGGRESSION: THE CLEAR MESSAGE FORMAT
  A. **Behavior**
  B. **Interpretation**
  C. **Feeling**
  D. **Consequence**
    1. What happens to you, the speaker
    2. What happens to the person you're addressing
    3. What happens to others

    E. **Intention**
      1. Where you stand on an issue
      2. Requests of others
      3. Descriptions of how you plan to act in the future

    F. **Using the Clear Message Format**
      1. No correct order
      2. Word to suit your style
      3. Combine elements
      4. May need repetition

IV. CONFLICT IN RELATIONAL SYSTEMS
    A. **Complementary, Symmetrical and Parallel Styles**
    B. **Intimate and Aggressive Styles**
    C. **Conflict Rituals**

V. VARIABLES IN CONFLICT STYLES
    A. **Gender**
    B. **Culture**

VI. METHODS OF CONFLICT RESOLUTION
    A. **Win–Lose**
    B. **Lose–Lose**
    C. **Compromise**
    D. **Win–Win**

VII. WIN–WIN COMMUNICATION SKILLS
    A. **Identify Your Problem and Unmet needs**
    B. **Make a Date**
    C. **Describe Your Problem and Needs**
    D. **Consider Your Partner's Point of View**
    E. **Negotiate a Solution**
    F. **Follow up the Solution**

VIII. CONSTRUCTIVE CONFLICT: QUESTIONS AND ANSWERS
    A. **Isn't Win–Win Too Good to Be True?**
    B. **Is It Possible to Change Others?**
    C. **Isn't Win–Win Negotiating Too Rational?**

▲ KEY TERMS

accommodation
aggressive conflict style
assertion
avoidance
behavioral description
clear message format
complementary conflict style
compromise
conflict
conflict ritual
consequence statement
crazymaking
direct aggression
ends
feeling statement
indirect aggression
indirect communication

intention statement
interpretation
intimate conflict style
lose–lose problem solving
negotiation
no-lose problem solving
nonassertion
parallel conflict style
passive aggression
relational conflict style
scarce rewards
struggle
symmetrical conflict style
win–lose problem solving
win–win problem solving
withholder

▲ 10.1 UNDERSTANDING CONFLICT STYLES

PURPOSE

To help you understand the styles with which conflicts can be handled.

INSTRUCTIONS

1. For each of the conflicts described below, write four responses illustrating nonassertive, directly aggressive, passive aggression, indirect communication, and assertive communication styles.
2. Describe the probable consequences of each style.

EXAMPLE

Three weeks ago your friend borrowed an article of clothing, promising to return it soon. You haven't seen it since, and the friend hasn't mentioned it.

Nonassertive response *Say nothing to the friend, hoping she will remember and return the item.*

Probable consequences *There's a good chance I'll never get the item back. I would probably resent the friend and avoid her in the future so I won't have to lend anything else.*

Directly aggressive response *Confront the friend and accuse her of being inconsiderate and irresponsible. Say that she probably ruined the item and is afraid to say so.*

Probable consequences *My friend would get defensive and hurt. Even if she did intentionally keep the item, she'd never admit it when approached this way. We would probably avoid each other in the future.*

Passive aggressive response *Complain to another friend, knowing it will get back to her.*

Probable consequences *My friend might be embarrassed by my gossip and be even more resistant to return it.*

Indirect communication *Drop hints about how I loved to wear the borrowed item. Casually mention how much I hate people who don't return things.*

Probable consequences *My friend might ignore my hints. She'll most certainly resent my roundabout approach, even if she returns the article.*

Assertive response *Confront the friend in a noncritical way and remind her that she still has the item. Ask when she'll return it, being sure to get a specific time.*

Probable consequences *The friend might be embarrassed when I bring the subject up, but since there's no attack it'll probably be okay. Since we'll have cleared up the problem, the relationship can continue.*

1. Someone you've just met at a party criticizes a mutual friend in a way you think is unfair.

   Nonassertive response _____

   _____

   _____

   _____

Probable consequences _____

_____

_____

_____

Directly aggressive response _____

_____

_____

_____

Probable consequences _____

_____

_____

_____

Passive aggressive response _____

_____

_____

_____

Probable consequences _____

_____

_____

_____

Indirect communication _____

_____

_____

_____

Probable consequences _____

_____

_____

_____

Assertive response _____

_____

_____

_____

Probable consequences _____

_____

_____

_____

2. A fan behind you at a ballgame toots a loud air horn every time the home team makes any progress. The noise is spoiling your enjoying of the game.

Nonassertive response _____

_____

_____

_____

Probable consequences _____

_____

_____

_____

Directly aggressive response _____

_____

_____

_____

Probable consequences _____

_____

_____

_____

Passive aggressive response _____

_____

_____

_____

Probable consequences _____

_____

_____

_____

Indirect communication _____

_____

_____

_____

Probable consequences _____

_____

_____

_____

Assertive response _____

_____

_____

_____

Probable consequences _____

_____

_____

_____

3. Earlier in the day you asked the person with whom you live to stop by the store and pick up snacks for a party you are having this evening. S/he arrives home without the food, and it's too late to return to the store.

Nonassertive response _____

_____

_____

_____

Probable consequences _____

_____

_____

_____

Directly aggressive response _____

_____

_____

_____

Probable consequences _____

_____

_____

_____

Passive aggressive response _____

_____

_____

_____

Probable consequences _____

_____

_____

_____

Indirect communication _____

_____

_____

_____

Probable consequences _____

_____

_____

_____

Assertive response _____

_____

_____

_____

Probable consequences _____

_____

_____

_____

4. You are explaining your political views to a friend who has asked your opinion. Now the friend obviously isn't listening. You think to yourself that since the person asked for your ideas, the least s/he can do is pay attention.

Nonassertive response _____

_____

_____

_____

Probable consequences _____

_____

_____

_____

Directly aggressive response _____

_____

_____

_____

Probable consequences _____

_____

_____

_____

Passive aggressive response _____

_____

_____

_____

Probable consequences _____

_____

_____

_____

Indirect communication _____

_____

_____

_____

Probable consequences _____

_____

_____

_____

Assertive response _____

_____

_____

_____

Probable consequences _____

_____

_____

_____

▲ 10.2 WRITING CLEAR MESSAGES

PURPOSE

To help you turn unclear messages into clear ones.

INSTRUCTIONS

Imagine a situation in which you might have said each of the statements below. Rewrite the messages in the clear message format, being sure to include each of the five elements described in your text.

EXAMPLE

Unclear message: "It's awful when you can't trust a friend."

Clear message:

Lena, when Jim told me he knew I went out with Warren,	(behavior)
I figured you'd told him.	(interpretation)
I'm embarrassed and disappointed	(feeling)
because I didn't want Jim to know.	(consequence)
Don't ever tell Jim when I go out with someone else.	(intention)

1. "Blast it, Robin! Get off my back."

_____	(behavior)
_____	(interpretation)
_____	(feeling)
_____	(consequence)
_____	(intention)

2. "I wish you'd pay more attention to me."

_____	(behavior)
_____	(interpretation)
_____	(feeling)
_____	(consequence)
_____	(intention)

3. "You've sure been thoughtful lately."

_____ (behavior)

_____ (interpretation)

_____ (feeling)

_____ (consequence)

_____ (intention)

4. "Nobody's perfect!"

_____ (behavior)

_____ (interpretation)

_____ (feeling)

_____ (consequence)

_____ (intention)

5. "Matt, you're such a slob!"

_____ (behavior)

_____ (interpretation)

_____ (feeling)

_____ (consequence)

_____ (intention)

6. "Let's just forget it; with all the screaming, I get flustered."

_____ (behavior)

_____ (interpretation)

_____ (feeling)

_____ (consequence)

_____ (intention)

7. "I really shouldn't eat any of that cake you baked."

_____ (behavior)

_____ (interpretation)

_____ (feeling)

_____ (consequence)

_____ (intention)

▲ 10.3 BUILDING CLEAR MESSAGES

PURPOSE

To help you develop clear, complete messages about important issues in your life.

INSTRUCTIONS

1. List five significant messages which you could send to important people in your life: complaints, requests, or expressions of appreciation.
2. Describe each message in terms of behavior.
3. For each message, record two possible interpretations.
4. After giving the matter some thought, circle the interpretation that is most realistic.
5. Record the feelings which follow from the circled interpretation.
6. Describe the consequences, for you and the other person involved, which flow from your interpretation.
7. List any intentions you have which result from the information you have recorded so far. Remember that you can have single or multiple intentions, which can involve either statements of where you stand, requests of others, or descriptions of how you plan to act in the future.

Message (behavior)	Interpretations		Feelings	Consequences		Intentions
	A	B		for you	for other	
Example When you comment about my "putting on a few pounds"	I think this is just an innocent remark.	I imagine you think I'm unattractive but you don't want to tell me directly.	Hurt; defensive	I wonder what else you dislike about me. I also get quiet and withdraw.	I'm not much fun to be with.	I want you to tell me outright whether you think I'm too heavy, so I don't have to guess.
1.						
2.						

Message (behavior)	Interpretations		Feelings	Consequences		Intentions
	A	B		for you	for other	
3.						
4.						
5.						

▲ 10.4 CHECKLIST FOR ORAL SKILL— BUILDING CLEAR MESSAGES

PURPOSE

To give you practice in building clear messages orally.

INSTRUCTIONS

Using the messages you created from your own personal experiences in *10.3 Building Clear Messages*, deliver a clear message to a partner. Identify and evaluate each of the elements of your message.

CHECKLIST

5 = superior   4 = excellent   3 = good   2 = fair   1 = poor

Exhibits appropriate nonverbal behaviors   _____
    —looks in the direction of other
    —tone of voice is nondefensive
    —faces partner

Delivers a clear message   _____

    —describes behavior   _____

    —gives at least one interpretation of behavior   _____

    —describes feelings   _____

    —describes at least one consequence   _____

    —indicates an intention   _____

Identifies and evaluates each of the elements of a clear message   _____

                                          Total   _____

▲ 10.5 YOUR CONFLICT STYLES

PURPOSE

To help you identify the styles you use to handle conflicts.

INSTRUCTIONS

1. Use the form below to record the conflicts which occur in your life. Describe any minor issues which arise as well as major problems.
2. For each incident, describe your conflict style, your approach to resolution, and the consequences of these behaviors.
3. Summarize your findings in the space provided.

Incident	Your Behavior	Your Conflict Style	Approach to Resolution	Consequences
Example My friend accused me of being too negative about the possibility of finding reward-ing, well-paying work.	I became defensive and angri-ly denied his claim. In turn I accused him of being too critical.	Direct aggression	Win–lose	After arguing for some time, we left each other, both feel-ing upset. I'm sure we'll both feel awkward around each other for a while.
1.				
2.				

Incident	Your Behavior	Your Conflict Style	Approach to Resolution	Consequences
3.				
4.				
5.				

CONCLUSIONS

Are there any individuals or issues which repeatedly arouse conflicts?

_____

_____

_____

What conflict style(s) do you most commonly use? Do you use different styles with different people or in different situations? Describe.

_____

_____

_____

_____

_____

_____

What approaches do you usually take in resolving conflicts? Do you use different approaches depending on the people or situations? Describe.

_____

_____

_____

_____

What are the consequences of the behaviors you described above? Are you satisfied with them? If not, how could you change?

_____

_____

_____

_____

_____

▲ 10.6 ANALYZING YOUR NEEDS

PURPOSES

1. To help you recognize that you initiate conflicts because you (not others) have problems.
2. To help you identify the ends you are seeking in personal conflicts, rather than focusing prematurely on one or more means to that end.
3. To help you better understand the ends (needs) others want to have met in your conflicts.

INSTRUCTIONS

1. Use the space below to record four incidents in which you were critical of another person's behavior.
2. In each case, describe the end you were seeking which seemed to be blocked by the other person's actions.
3. Now try to understand the end which the other person was seeking by behaving as s/he did. If possible, you should ask the other person to identify these ends. Why guess when you can know for sure?

Your Complaint	The Unmet Need (End) That Prompted Your Complaint	The Other's Unmet Need (End) Which Led to the Behavior (Did You Ask?)
Example My family writes nagging letters complaining that I "never write or phone them."	To have them not treat me as a child, asking for information which I want to keep private and offering advice which makes me feel they don't think I can make decisions on my own.	To know how I'm doing. To know that I'm thinking about them and still love them. (I asked them, which they appreciated.)
1.		
2.		
3.		

Your Complaint	The Unmet Need (End) That Prompted Your Complaint	The Other's Unmet Need (End) Which Led to the Behavior (Did You Ask?)
4.		
5.		

NAME _____

▲ 10.7 WIN–WIN PROBLEM SOLVING

PURPOSE

To help you apply the win–win problem solving method to a personal conflict.

INSTRUCTIONS

1. Follow the instructions below as a guide to dealing with an interpersonal conflict facing you now. Realize that you needn't choose an issue of critical importance; the method works well on relatively minor issues too.
2. After completing the no-lose steps, record your conclusions in the space provided.

Step 1: Identify your unmet needs (ends you are seeking).

_____

_____

_____

_____

Step 2: Make a date. (Choose a time and place which will make it easiest for both parties to work constructively on the issue.)

_____

_____

_____

_____

Step 3: Describe your problem and needs. (Use behavior—interpret—feel—consequence—intend format, but avoid proposing specific means or solutions at this point.)

_____

_____

_____

_____

Step 4: Consider your partner's point of view. (Ask your partner what s/he wants and check your understanding—paraphrase or perception—check as necessary.)

_____

_____

_____

_____

Step 5: Negotiate a solution.

a. Restate the needs of both parties, just to be sure they are clear.

_____

_____

_____

_____

b. Work together to generate a number of possible solutions (means) which might satisfy these needs. Don't criticize any suggestions here!

_____

_____

_____

_____

_____

_____

c. Evaluate the solutions you just listed, considering the advantages and problems of each. If you think of any new solutions, record them above.

d. Decide on the best solution, listing it here.

_____

_____

_____

_____

Step 6: Follow up the solution. After a trial period, meet with your partner and see if your agreement is satisfying both your needs. If not, return to step 3 and use this procedure to refine your solution.

_____

_____

_____

_____

CONCLUSIONS

In what ways did this procedure differ from the way in which you usually deal with interpersonal conflicts?

_____

_____

_____

_____

_____

Was the outcome of your problem solving session different from what it might have been if you had communicated in your usual style? How?

_____

_____

_____

_____

In what ways can you use the no-lose methods in your interpersonal conflicts? With whom? On what issues? What kinds of behavior will be especially important?

_____

_____

_____

_____

_____

▲ 10.8 ORAL SKILL—CONFLICT RESOLUTION DYADS

PURPOSE

To develop your skills in using the assertive, win–win conflict resolution methods introduced in Chapter 10 of *Looking Out/Looking In.*

INSTRUCTIONS

1. Join with three partners and identify the members as A, B, C, and D.
2. A and B choose an issue from the list below and role-play simulated conflict, using the assertive, win–win conflict resolution methods introduced in Chapter 10 of *Looking Out/Looking In.*
3. During the role-playing situation, C uses *10.10 Checklist for Oral Skill—Conflict Resolution Dyads* to evaluate A's communication skill, while D uses the checklist to evaluate B's skill.
4. After the role-play, C provides feedback to A, and D provides feedback to B.
5. Switch roles so that C and D role-play a conflict, while A and B complete the checklist and provide feedback to C and D.

ISSUES FOR CONFLICT RESOLUTION DYADS

Choose one of the following issues and supply details as necessary for the conflict resolution dyad role-play. Partners may substitute another issue if they choose.

> household chores
> academic grades
> budgeting
> use of language offensive to one partner
> exclusive vs. nonexclusive dating or friendships
> use of alcohol, drugs, etc.
> how much time to spend with/apart from one another
> parental involvement in offspring's life
> use of equipment or clothing belonging to one partner

▲ 10.9 CHECKLIST FOR ORAL SKILL—
CONFLICT RESOLUTION DYADS

PURPOSE

To provide feedback to others concerning their effectiveness in using win–win conflict resolution methods.

INSTRUCTIONS

Use the following rating system to evaluate the respondent in each area according to the situations developed in *10.9 Oral Skill —Conflict Resolution Dyads.*

CHECKLIST

5 = superior   4 = excellent   3 = good   2 = fair   1 = poor

Identifies own unmet needs   _____

Makes a date   _____

Describes problem and needs   _____
        —behavior
        —interpretations
        —feelings
        —consequences
        —intentions

Considers partner's point of view/solicits partner's understanding   _____

Paraphrases/perception checks to verify understanding of partner's needs   _____

Negotiates win–win solution to best possible extent   _____
        —identifies/summarizes conflict
        —generates possible solutions without premature evaluation
        —evaluates alternatives
        —decides on win–win solution

Plans follow-up meeting to modify solution as necessary.   _____

                                                    Total   _____

▲ 10.10 IDENTIFYING CLEAR MESSAGE ELEMENTS

PURPOSE

To help you recognize the elements of a clear message.

INSTRUCTIONS

Identify which element of a clear message is being used in each statement according to the following key:

a. behavioral description
b. interpretation
c. feeling
d. consequence
e. intention

_____ 1. That's a good idea.

_____ 2. I'm worried about this course.

_____ 3. Jim looked angry today.

_____ 4. I want to talk to you about the $20 you borrowed.

_____ 5. I notice that you haven't been smiling much lately.

_____ 6. I don't know whether you're serious or not.

_____ 7. I'm glad you invited me.

_____ 8. Ever since then I've found myself avoiding you.

_____ 9. I'm sorry you didn't like my work.

_____ 10. I want you to know how important this is to me.

_____ 11. It looks to me like you meant to embarrass me.

_____ 12. "... and after that you seemed to withdraw."

_____ 13. I see you're wearing my ring again.

_____ 14. From now on you can count on me.

_____ 15. You've never said anything like that before.

_____ 16. ... and since then I've been sleeping at my dad's house.

▲ 10.11 IDENTIFYING PERSONAL CONFLICT STYLES

PURPOSE

To give you practice in identifying personal conflict styles.

INSTRUCTIONS

1. Match the letter of the personal conflict style with its description found below.
2. Check your answers in the back of this manual on page 282.

   a. avoidance
   b. accommodation
   c. direct aggression
   d. assertion
   e. indirect communication
   f. passive aggression

_____ 1. Stan keeps joking around to keep us from talking about commitment.

_____ 2. "I can't believe you were so stupid as to have erased the disk."

_____ 3. Even though he wanted to go to the party, Allen stayed home with Sara rather than hear her complain.

_____ 4. By mentioning how allergic she was to smoke, Joan hoped that her guest would smoke outside.

_____ 5. "When you smoke inside, I start to cough and my eyes water, so please go out on the balcony when you want to smoke."

_____ 6. Rather than tell Nick about his frustration over Nick not meeting the deadline, Howard complained to others about Nick's unreliability while maintaining a smiling front to Nick.

_____ 7. Carol wouldn't answer the phone after their disagreement because she was afraid it would be Nancy on the other end.

_____ 8. Faced with his obvious distress, Nikki put her very important work aside to listen to him.

_____ 9. Even though Nikki could see Kham's distress, she told him she had a deadline to meet in one hour and asked if they could talk then.

_____ 10. (Sarcastically) "Oh, sure, I *loved* having dinner with your parents instead of going to the party Saturday night."

▲ ANSWER KEY ▲

1.11 IDENTIFYING THE COMMUNICATION PROCESS

1. c	2. a	3. b	4. e	5. f
6. e	7. g	8. d	9. b	10. c
11. g	12. e	13. a	14. a	15. d

2.10 IDENTIFYING ASPECTS OF THE SELF-CONCEPT

1. a	2. c	3. d	4. b	5. b
6. c	7. a	8. d	9. c	10. b

3.11 RECOGNIZING PERCEPTION-CHECKING ELEMENTS

1. b	2. b	3. a	4. c	5. d
6. c	7. b	8. b	9. a	10. d

4.2 FIND THE FEELINGS

1. This statement certainly implies some kind of positive feeling, but doesn't tell us clearly what it is.
2. The speaker here is labeling another's feelings, but saying nothing about his/her own. Is the speaker concerned, irritated, or indifferent to the other person's suspected sensitivity? We don't know.
3. The emotion here is implied but not stated. The speaker might be frustrated, perplexed, or tired.
4. Here is a clear statement of the speaker's emotional state.
5. We know the speaker loves the helpfulness, but does s/he love the helper or simply feel gratitude? Love is probably not an accurate description of the emotion, in any case.
6. Just because we say "I feel" doesn't mean a feeling is being expressed. This is an interpretation statement.
7. How does the speaker feel about the hopeless situation: resigned, sad, desperate? We haven't been told.
8. Again, no feeling stated. Is the speaker worried, afraid, distraught?
9. This could be a statement of concern, irritation, or genuine confusion. Nonverbal clues can help us decide, but a feeling statement would tell us for certain.
10. Here's a metaphorical statement of feeling, strongly suggesting surprise or shock. This sort of message probably does an adequate job of expressing the emotion here, but it might be too vague for some people to understand.

4.10 IDENTIFYING IRRATIONAL FALLACIES

1. a	2. f	3. c	4. b	5. g
6. d	7. d	8. c	9. g	10. a
11. e	12. e	13. f	14. b	

5.13 IDENTIFYING LANGUAGE TYPES

1. a	2. c	3. b	4. d	5. e
6. c	7. e	8. c	9. a	10. d
11. c	12. b	13. b	14. d	

5.14 IDENTIFYING ABSTRACT LANGUAGE

1. c	2. a	3. b	4. d	5. a

6.12 IDENTIFYING TYPES OF NONVERBAL COMMUNICATION

1. a	2. d	3. e	4. c	5. a
6. b	7. b	8. b	9. c	10. d
11. e	12. a	13. c	14. d	

7.11 IDENTIFYING INFORMATIONAL PARAPHRASING RESPONSES

1. c	2. a	3. c	4. d	5. a

7.12 IDENTIFYING PARAPHRASING FOR PROBLEM SOLVING

1. d	2. a	3. c	4. b	5. d

7.13 IDENTIFYING TYPES OF LISTENING

1. f	2. g	3. c	4. d	5. b
6. a	7. a	8. g	9. b	10. f
11. d	12. e	13. b	14. a	15. g

8.10 IDENTIFYING DEVELOPMENTAL STAGES

1. e	2. a	3. c	4. b	5. f
6. h	7. g	8. d	9. i	10. j

9.8 IDENTIFYING DEFENSIVENESS AND SUPPORTIVENESS

1. f	2. l	3. d	4. j	5. k
6. c	7. e	8. i	9. h	10. b
11. a	12. g	13. c	14. e	

10.11 IDENTIFYING PERSONAL CONFLICT STYLES

1. a	2. c	3. b	4. e	5. d
6. f	7. a	8. b	9. d	10. f